THE *bigbook* OF
twenty-five
HOUSES

THE *bigbook* OF

twenty-five
HOUSES

AUTHOR

Francisco Asensio Cerver

PUBLISHING DIRECTOR

Nacho Asensio

PROJECT COORDINATOR

Ivan Bercedo (Architect)

TRANSLATION

Mark Lodge

PROOFREADING

Amber Okrassa, Elaine Fradley, Judy Thomson

GRAPHIC DESIGN

Mireia Casanovas Soley Noemí Blanco

LAYOUT

Òscar Lleonart Ruiz

TEXTS

Ivan Bercedo: Introduction, House in Los Vilos, O Residence, House in Tateshina, Coll-Vallés House, Schöener House, House in Bosque de Las Lomas, House in Querétaro, Stampfel House, Bielicky House, Duffy House.
Cayetano Cardelús: House in Collserola.
Ramon Esteve: House in Na Xemena.
Finn Kappe: Kappe Tamuri Residence.
Grupo LBC: House in Celaya.
Itziar Sen: Stremmel Residence, Villa in the Forest.
Judy Thomson: Rosenthal House, The Flower House, Susman Bay House, Collective Housing for the Cheesecake Consortium, Barnes House, Poole Residence, Linear House, Type/Variant House, Villa Wilbrink, Capistrano Beach House.

Copyright © 2000 Francisco Asensio Cerver

Published by: Atrium International
Ganduxer 115, 4º
Barcelona 08022 Spain.
Phone +34-93-418 49 10 Fax +34-93-211 81 39
E-mail:arcoedit@idgrup.ibernet.com
Dep. Leg.: B-45461/99
ISBN: 84-8185-232-5
Printed in Spain

An architect who is commissioned such a personal project as designing a house knows that their plans must meet the owner's needs and realize their dreams. This influences all the design process because the architect has to make real the client's dream of having a unique, made-to-measure private space in which to live.

In the projects selected for this book it can be seen that the architects have borne this in mind. The aim is to show a sample of twenty-five houses designed by prestigious architect like Mark Mack, Gabriel Poole, Wolfgang Döring, J. Frank Fitzgibbons, and John and Patricia Patkau. Other, less known, creators are included. They will surely be acclaimed as their works come to the attention of the critics. All of them got the most out of their creativity to conceive these houses which manifest the latest vogues in home design. The results can be seen in the beautiful photographs.

Names like Ben van Berkel, Kazuyo Sejima, Rob Wellington Quigley, and Fernau and Hartman, all of which have earned themselves fame over the recent years, are also represented in this book. The houses they designed are spread right across the world: the United States, Chile, Germany, Japan, the United Kingdom, Mexico, Holland and Spain. This offers the reader an unbeatable panorama of worldwide home design.

Just leafing through these pages is enough to realize that each house style has its own subtle differences. Not only are the personalities of the architect and the owners stamped on a house. The environment, the landscape and the climate leave their indelible mark on its design. Therefore, the book has been divided into six sections: houses in the city, houses in the country, houses in the mountains, houses even higher up in the mountains, and houses on the outskirts. In this final chapter we have grouped together the houses that although they are within city limits are free from the constraints that impact on city houses: noise, pollution and lack of space. The reader will see that even in such hostile surroundings the architect can construct genuine works of art.

The houses in this book have been carefully selected because of their beauty and style. They appear straightforward but they have been meticulously thought out so as to blend in with the landscape and to make them easy to live in. A sensation of spaciousness is given by all of them. Some are austerely decorated, or have a straight-line, hard edge design that plays with the light. The stunning photographs let the reader in on some of the designer's intentions and means for achieving effects, enabling the project to be understood.

In summary, the BigBook of Twenty-five Houses offers a sample of those kind of homes that make us desire one just the same. However, this dream can never come true because the house we admire reflects someone else's personality. Houses are more intimate than we realize.

THE *bigbook* OF

twenty-five
HOUSES

The Flower Housel

Peter Romaniuk

Judging by the number of contemporary architects who cite the "Case Study" houses built in California in the fifties and sixties as the source of their inspiration, they must stand high in any ranking of :"Great Architectural Influences of today."

In this case, London architect Peter Romaniuk was not faced with uneven desert terrain, or a sloping hillside; there were not even magnificent views that had to be maximised, but the concept was still appropriate. Romaniuk and his wife, Paula Pryke, had acquired a very tight urban site in a typical Victorian street in central London to build their own home; it also had to accommodate a workshop where Pryke, an internationally recognised florist, could work and run a flower school.

They were keen to have as much light as can be achieved in the midst of an urban setting without relinquishing privacy. Like generations of designers faced with a brief for an individual house, Peter Romaniuk claims he was greatly influenced by the "Case Study" houses built by architects such as Neutra and Koenig.

The house is a modern steel-framed building with a workshop on the ground floor and a two-story residence above. The proximity of neighbors is inevitable in such a central location in London, where terraced houses look onto each other across the street and through their rear windows, but not unavoidable as Romaniuk ingeniously shows. He designed the house so they could figuratively turn their back on the neighbors. It faces one way, to the East, in a radical move away from the traditional front and rear of most housing. Also as the residential part of the building begins on the first floor and is set back, the home is one stage removed from street bustle.

The substantial first-floor terrace, giving on to the street, reinforces the inner privacy but at the same time is an appealing outlet, a rare luxury for an inner-city property. The plan is fiercely simple and rational. The architect was determined the building structure should be clearly expressed. He created a modular system that suited both the work space and home, and the different elements – walls, ceiling, floor, steel frame, stairs... – are all treated in the same way. The result is a homogeneous building with esthetic and structural echoes between workshop and residence, and between first and second floors.

The structural steel frame is set on a 3.6 x 3.6 meter grid. Mies-style cruciform columns are bolted to twin back-to-back steel angle beams. There is a certain pragmatic nature to this house, seen in various aspects but neatly illustrated by one detail of its construction: the beams were split to reduce their weight so two men could handle them, thereby avoiding the expense and inconvenience of a crane. The member sizes were carefully chosen for their good Hp/A factors to reduce the thickness of the instrument coating to a minimum. Two layers of profiled steel decking riveted together at right angles span the structural frame and create a two-way spanning floor system. The desire transparency has been achieved by the large, open spaces on every level, and the full height sliding glass panels giving on to the terrace and second-floor balcony. The solid rear wall is used for the storage. The interior spaces are clear and unobstructed, and circulation and living areas almost merge. The landing or hall on the second floor is just punctuated by circular pods with overhead skylights, containing bath, dressing area and shower; they are like sculptural features in the open space.

Planners who give building permission are beginning to be more flexible in London, after a period since the early eighties when modern architecture was seriously restricted, but it is still not common. Just as Michael Hopkins, whose highly regarded practice Romaniuk is an associate of, stood out among his generation for his own totally uncompromising house, so has Peter Romaniuk achieved a significant feat by building an utterly modern house in this urban context.

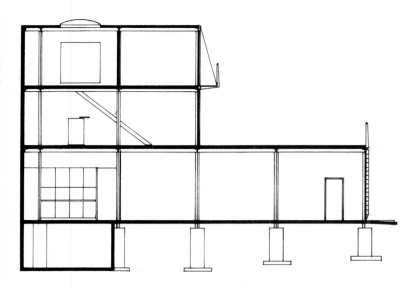

Cross section.

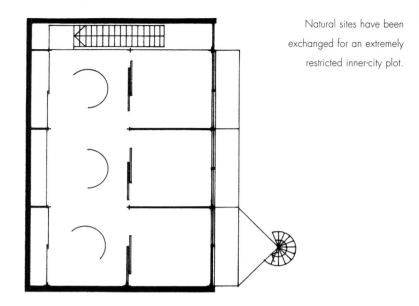

Natural sites have been exchanged for an extremely restricted inner-city plot.

Ground floor.

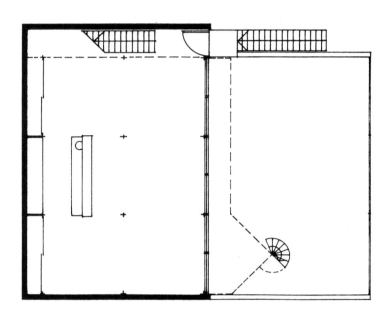

First floor.

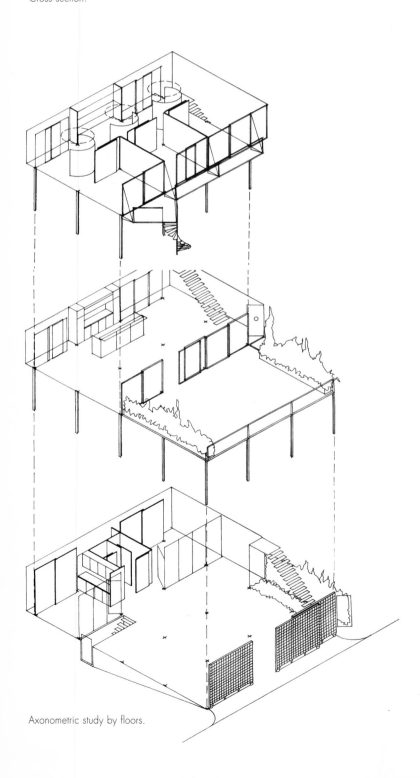

Axonometric study by floors.

Second floor.

Detail plan of the steel staircase
which leads from the living room
to bedroom level. Many
elements in this house give it an
industrial feel: the staircase, the
exposed concrete walls (just
painted) or the galvanized steel
roof. At the same time there is
an immediacy and honesty in its
construction.

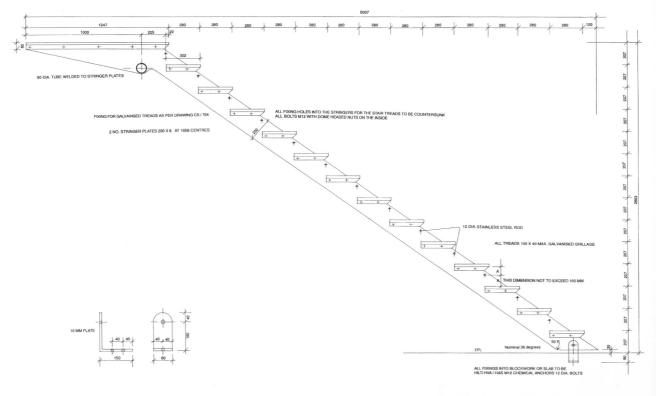

90 DIA. TUBE WELDED TO STRINGER PLATES

FIXING FOR GALVAINSED TREADS AS PER DRAWING CS / 704

2 NO. STRINGER PLATES 200 X 8   AT 1058 CENTRES

ALL FIXING HOLES INTO THE STRINGERS FOR THE STAIR TREADS TO BE COUNTERSUNK
ALL BOLTS M12 WITH DOME HEADED NUTS ON THE INSIDE

10 DIA. STAINLESS STEEL ROD

ALL TREADS 100 X 40 MAX. GALVANISED GRILLAGE

THIS DIMENSION NOT TO EXCEED 100 MM

Nominal 36 degrees

10 MM PLATE

FFL

ALL FIXINGS INTO BLOCKWORK OR SLAB TO BE
HILTI HVA / HAS M12 CHEMICAL ANCHORS 12 DIA. BOLTS

The kitchen is in a self standing
bar module along the wall
which encloses the rear of the
house. All the kitchen
components are stainless steel:
the work-surface, cupboards,
refrigerator and oven.

On the following pages:
Two views of the central
hallway of the top floor; the
different bathroom elements are
located independently
undermeanth three skylights
which let in natural light.

13

The Flower House

Location: London, United Kingdom.

Completion date: 1997.

Architects: Peter Romaniuk.

Collaborators: Tim McFarlane (structure), Jeff Parkes (installations), Ralph Pryke Partnership (constructor).

Photographer: Dennis Gilbert/VIEW.

e Flower House

House The Flower House

wer House

e The Flower House

wer House

House The Flower House The Flower House

r House The Flower House

e Flower House

The Flower House The Flower House

e Flower House

ower House

wer House

ower House The Flower House

House The Flower House

OOST GEVEL

Ben van Berkel

In this small family house situated in a district of Amersfoort in the Netherlands, architect Ben van Berkel has turned a few traditional notions about suburban housing upside-down. No rose garden, no lawn to mow, no views across the street, no neighbors peering in. A salutary solution to life on the outskirts perhaps. Certainly one would not expect anything less from Ben van Berkel and Caroline Bos, the dynamic partnership from Amsterdam, responsible for some profound explorations of architectural theory in recent years and the realization of some high-profile projects, including the Erasmus Bridge in Rotterdam.

It was apparently the client's aversion to gardening that played an important part in the design. As the architects comment:"The house was stretched out, using up as much land as possible with a limited programme, so as to avoid the presence of a garden." As a result the roof begins at the outer limit of the plot at street level and rises gently in an oblique plane. The only concession to a garden is a patch of shingle at the rear of the house, where some low-maintenance trees are planted in regimented fashion.

The oblique roof planes, covered in chunky, industrial gravel, present an austere appearance to the outsider, revealing little of the domestic life within. One feels the inhabitants are hunkering down inside this protective outer layer, like an animal within its shell. The different angles of the slope down to the garage and the upward slope of the roof reinforce this impression.

Once inside though there is an unexpected luminosity and clarity. The entrance, concealed in the middle of the oblique planes, is approached by a narrow path running between the garage and one of the gravel-covered slopes which leads to an inner courtyard. This is the core of the house: the quite small dwelling space is arranged in an L-shape around it. The hall leads directly into dining/kitchen area and on to living room which gives on to the rear; the bedroom wing, with a raised floor level to distinguish it, runs along the rear of the house. Within the privacy of the courtyard the extensive use of glass allows the natural light into the interior. Apart from a large, slanting window in the north facade, the outward-looking windows in the living area function more as interesting graphic features than for illumination, carefully designed to preserve privacy: an oblique horizontal strip in the kitchen parallels the sloping roof; a floor-level window in the living room becomes a focal point. The bedroom windows protrude slightly, encased in wood, disrupting the impeccably smooth surface of the rear wall, while an eye-level slit in the exterior wood-clad bathroom wall makes it an intriguing presence in the patio.

The exterior walls are clad in sand-limestone bricks which are glued rather than pointed. The effect is of a tough, rugged structure which combined with the gravel gives a very textured apparence. The interior provides a soothing contrast, with its smooth surfaces, light colored wood and minimal decoration.

This inward-looking contemporary urban patio house shuns its external surroundings to focus better on the life within it. Unlike many contemporary suburban properties, which are put on a pedestal for public admiration, Villa Wilbrink seems to have a more genuine response.

Villa Wilbrink

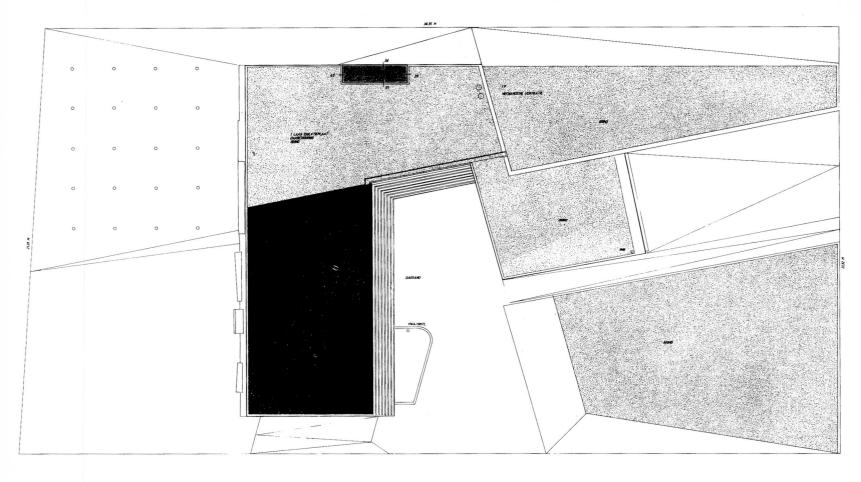

Plan of the roof.

Elevations.

View of the ramp
leading into the
garage.

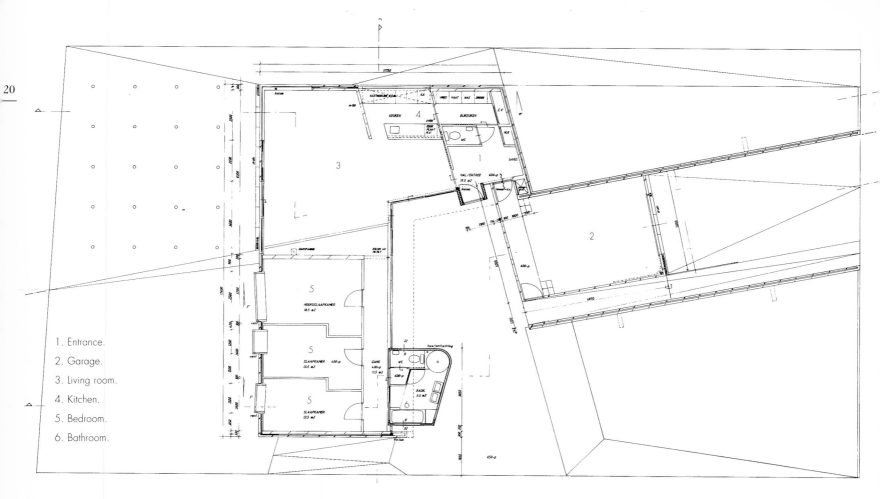

1. Entrance.
2. Garage.
3. Living room.
4. Kitchen.
5. Bedroom.
6. Bathroom.

Ground floor plan.

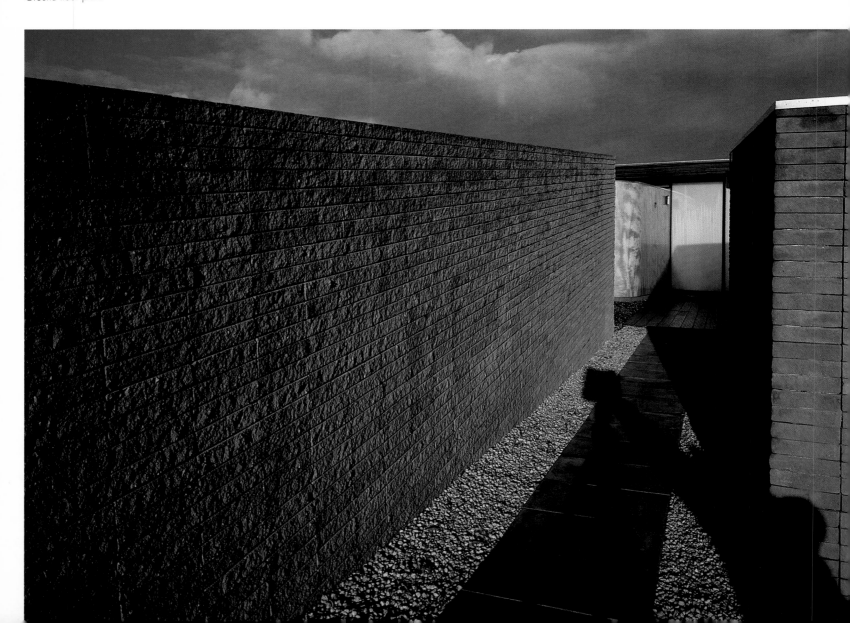

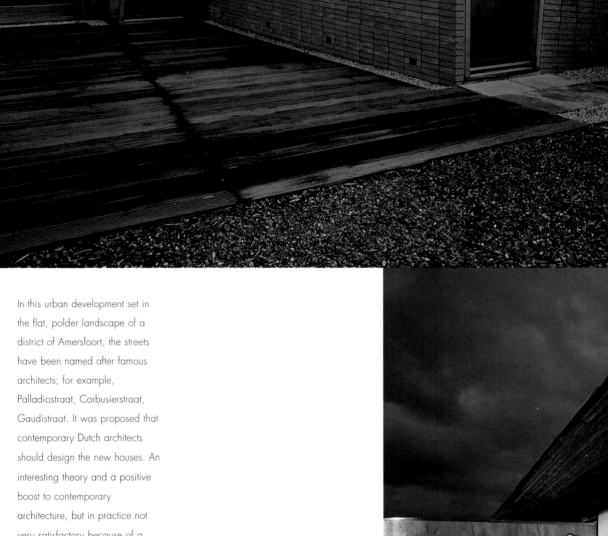

In this urban development set in the flat, polder landscape of a district of Amersfoort, the streets have been named after famous architects; for example, Palladiostraat, Corbusierstraat, Gaudistraat. It was proposed that contemporary Dutch architects should design the new houses. An interesting theory and a positive boost to contemporary architecture, but in practice not very satisfactory because of a lack of cohesion. Villa Wilbrink has a bold self-sufficiency which perhaps explains why it is one of the more successful results of this initiative.

The house's orthogonal system defined by the sloping roof rather than the horizontal floor has prompted comparisons with Frank Lloyd Wright's Taliesin West and its relationship with the Arizona desert. Villa Wilbrink has created a distinctive landscape of its own.

Detail of the wooden
canopy.

The rear facade wall is
perpendicular to the roof, which
makes it lean slightly from the
vertical. This geometric effect
creates the impression that the
house is actually twisted, and
that this is why it is set below
street level.

Sections.

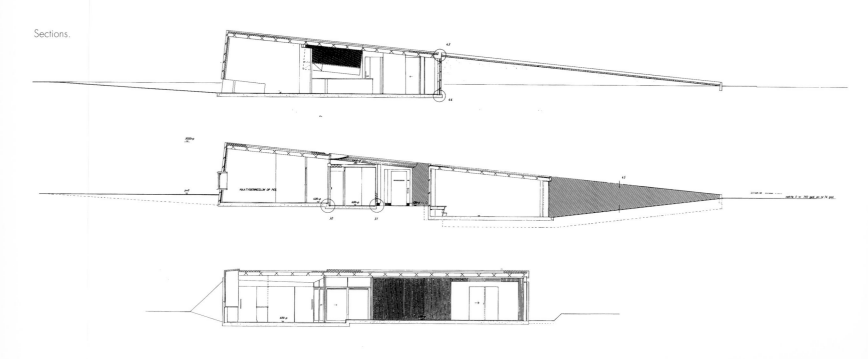

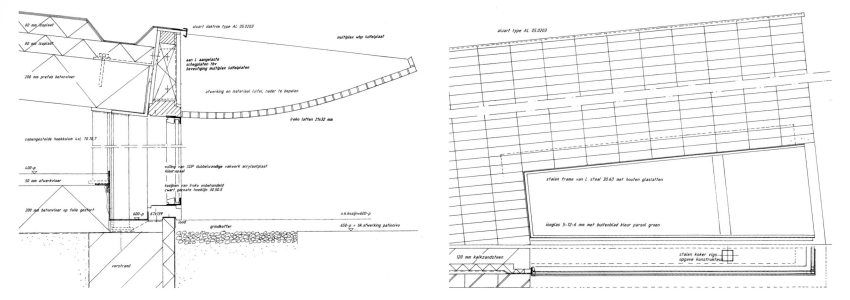

Detail of the window at floor level in the northern corner of the living room.

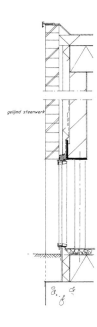

In the architect's words, "this modest family house is partially dictated by the client's hatred of gardening. The house was stretched out, using up as much land as possible with a limited programme, so as to avoid the presence of a garden".

The bright, light interiors with their clean lines and simple, sequential progress are a surprising contrast to the dour, grey appearance of the exteriors.

Villa Wilbrink

Location: A. Aaltostraat, Ameersfoort, Netherlands.

Completion date: 1994.

Architect: Ben van Berkel.

Collaborators: Aad Krom (project coordinator),
Paul van der Erve, Branimir Medic (design team),
BV Aannemingsmaatschappij ABM, Bureau
Bouwpartners (consultants).

Photographers: Hélène Bisnet, Kim Zwarts.

O Residence

Iida Archiship Studio

This house located in Tokyo was built for a young couple in their thirties. The surrounding neighborhood is a mixture of single-family homes in various styles and sizes, along with garages and various commercial buildings. There is no common standard for all of these constructions, and the result is a place where anything is possible although nothing is ever definitive.

Faced with this aggressive environment, Yoshihiko Iida chose to construct an introverted and introspected house with its own private and intimate environment. To achieve this, he includes exterior spaces within the house itself. This brings three main assets to the construction. First and most importantly, the rooms all have their own lighting and ventilation. Secondly, the architect has complete control over the views from the house, since all the rooms look out onto spaces which he himself has designed. And finally, these patios constitute ideal places for living outdoors, when the weather permits.

The house lies on an L- shaped lot, with another house to the west, the access road to the north, another lot to the south, and a narrow alley to the east. The shape of Iida's house is due to the fact that it partly surrounds the neighboring residence. Although there is very little distance between the two, they are not separated by a wall.

Iida has placed the three patios in strategic locations in the lot. One lies at the entrance, another at the point where the two wings of the house meet, and the third is found at one end. The garage is an independent construction which lies parallel to the street and protects the front yard from the inquisitive eyes of passersby. This creates an alternating pattern of constructed and "empty" spaces: garage, front patio, living room, central patio, bedroom, and back yard. It is obvious that the patios are of prime importance in determining both the distribution of the house and the daily life of its inhabitants.

Like two of the other city houses included in this book, Duffy House and Rosenthal House, a private landscape has been constructed with the inclusion of patios, gardens and yards, which affect not only the spatial arrangement of the house, but also its sense of time. Visitors or inhabitants must follow a route from the entrance of the house to the more private areas, passing along the way through several landscapes, each with its own identity. When the owners of the "O" residence go from the bedroom to the kitchen, they have the feeling of having left one place and entered another. This seems obvious, but it is actually rare in urban residences, where the confined spaces and homogenous decoration of the various rooms destroy the effect of change and movement.

The variety that springs from these different landscapes and the various levels on which the house is arranged mirrors the diversity of the surrounding city of Tokyo. The paradox lies in the fact that they are actually opposites: whereas the interior diversity is controlled and enriches the concept of the project, the exterior diversity is arbitrary and a source of disorder and confusion.

O Residence

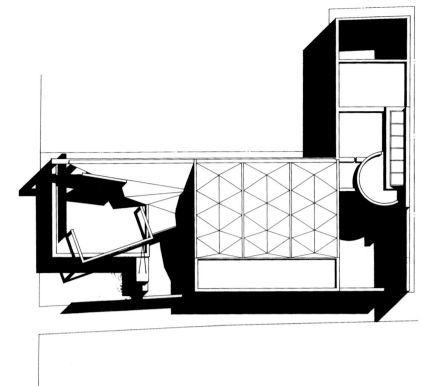

Views of the entrance from the street and from the front yard. The main floor is elevated from street level to increase the visual and acoustic isolation from the street. The garage acts as a screen to protect the front yard as well as the interior.

View of the living room roof from the patio which lies on top of the garage.

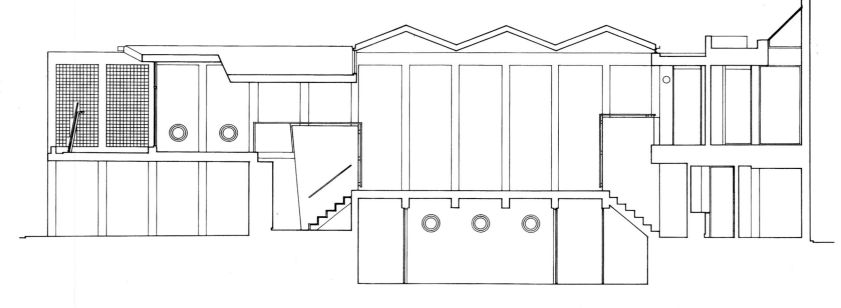

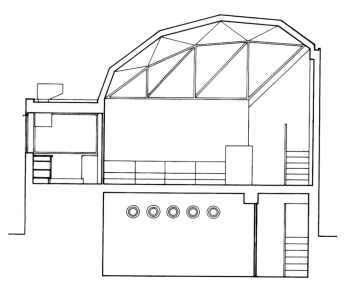

Cross section at the
living room.

Longitudinal section along
the main wing of the
building. The house is
distributed in two levels, one
of which is partly
underground.

The semi-arched roof, the
abundant natural light and
the spaciousness of the room
make it look almost like an
antdoor space or one of the
house's various patios.

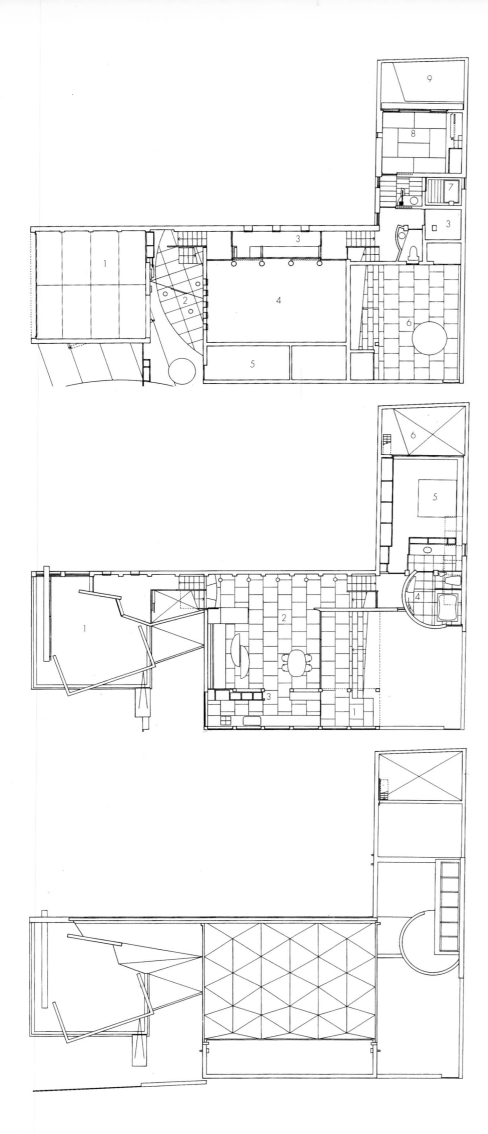

Semi-basement.

1. Garage.
2. Front patio.
3. Storage room.
4. Multi-purpose room.
5. Room for the water heater and other machines.
6. Patio.
7. Bathroom.
8. Tatami.
9. Patio.

Ground floor.

1. Patio.
2. Living room/dining room.
3. Kitchen.
4. Bathroom.
5. Master bedroom.
6. Empty space.

Plan of the roof.

The Semi-arche roof, the abundant natural light and spacionsness of the room (particulary for a country like Japan) make this space look almost like the ontdoors or a conered patio, very similar to the private patios actually existing in the house.

On the next page:

Two views of the tatami room

and the master bedroom.

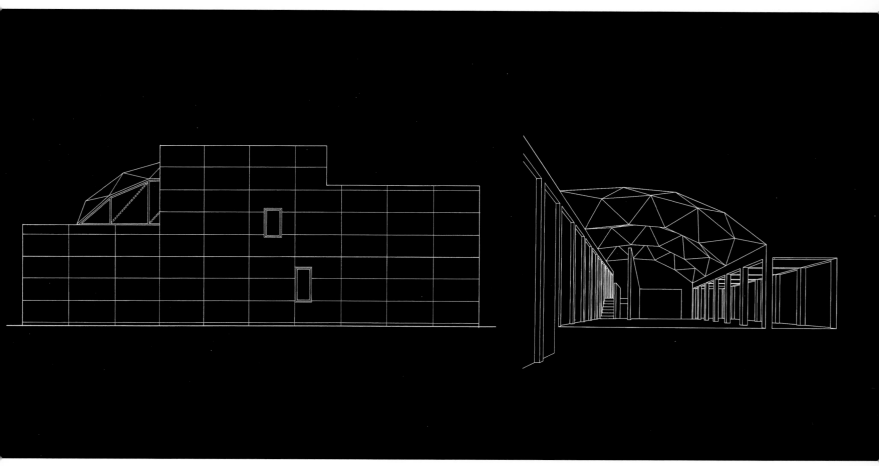

O Residence

Location: Tokyo, Japan.

Completion date: 1994.

Architect: Yoshihiko Iida.

Collaborators: SIGLO Structural Engineering (structure), Dan Mechanical Engineering (mechanical), Fuji-ken (construction).

Photographer: Koumei Tanaka

Duffy House

Bercedo + Mestre

The project consists of the refurbishing and enlargement of a small house located between party walls. The house was humid and in extremely bad condition, and consisted of one floor with a central hallway and small rooms on either side. It is located on an urban lot about 7 yards wide, between a four-story building on one side and a three-story building on the other.

In spite of the limitations of its location, the project manages to create an intimate environment containing a variety of different settings. Each space has a precise and identifiable ambiance, which manages to establish its own relationship with the inhabitants that pass through it. The architects propose a kind of game between memory and architecture, in which the former makes routes and the latter creates specific scenes. This game is only possible if the cards are not marked, which means that the shapes used must be simple and left bare.

Part of the framework of the old house was demolished to make space for an interior patio located just at the entrance. This creates a halfway point between the inside and the outside, which contrasts with the rather hermetic street façade. As a result, a visitor coming from the outside finds himself in a strange, unpredictable place. After this initial paradox, several routes take shape, alternating interior spaces with exterior ones and giving rise to unusual visual contrasts and complex situations.

A trip through the house involves a constant coming and going between interior and exterior. Precisely because the house is sandwiched between the surrounding buildings, the architects wanted to create a private exterior space that would allow the inhabitants to live outdoors. The various patios and terraces allow the house to breathe without opening onto the street, while at the same time creating a private territory with different levels and perspectives. Sunny areas alternate with shady ones, and the sun filters in through various cracks. The house even has a lookout point with a view of the sea.

As we pass through the terraces which climb like stairs from the ground floor to the third floor, peering through the skylights and openings that connect its different parts, the house begins to build itself in our memory. Many of the situations are incomprehensible until they are experienced directly, such as when we try to stick our heads out through an opening or pause for a moment on a narrow balcony. One of the differences between architecture and the other arts is its ability to incorporate seemingly trivial situations. There is no tuning up, no curtain raising before the show begins. For this reason its strategy must be extremely selective.

This method of creation springs from two convictions. In architecture, quick solutions and arbitrary images become dated just as quickly as their conception. Spaces should affect the people who inhabit them, but they must do so in a subtle way. What is essential is not spectacular effects, but the ability to accompany daily activity and fill it with magic by connecting it to the environment, to the position of the sun at each moment and to changing seasons.

Bercedo and Mestre cut a small opening in the wall for the sole purpose of allowing people to look out at the street when they wake up, or so that the sun will peep through at dawn. They place a window at the eye level of a sitting person so that it will frame the leaves of a tree as they read a book. These are ways of connecting individual and universal situations, so that these routine activities become less banal and more complete. The reflections of these activities, and other possible ones, are recorded on the walls, terraces and patios of the house. This, and very little else, is what architecture is all about.

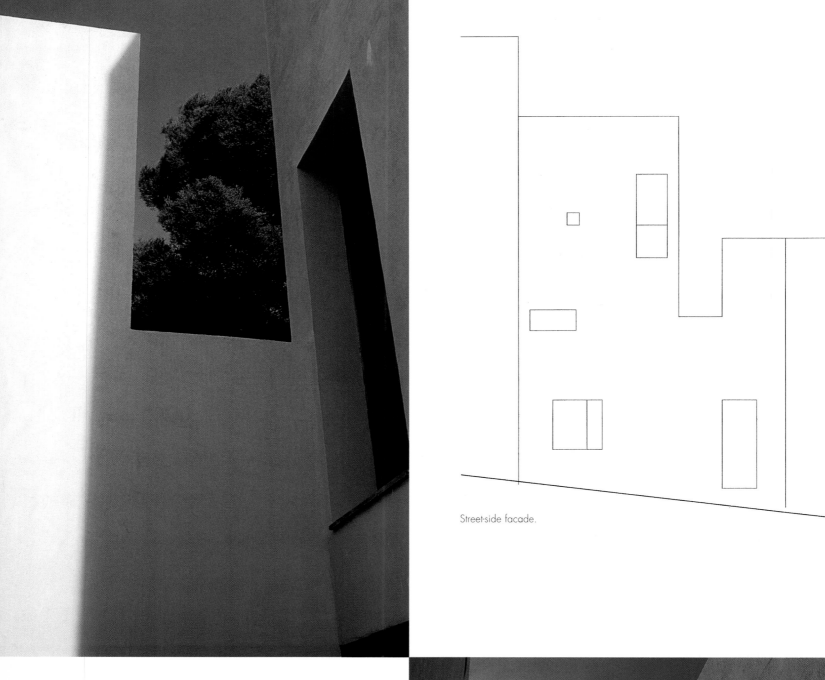

Street-side facade.

The house is almost totally isolated from the street. Not only is the façade hermetic, but the patio near the entrance functions as a kind of decompression chamber between the city and the residence.

The patio, living room and terrace that face the back yard are visually interconnected. Nevertheless, they each have their own lighting and personality. This creates the effect of three different layouts in one image.

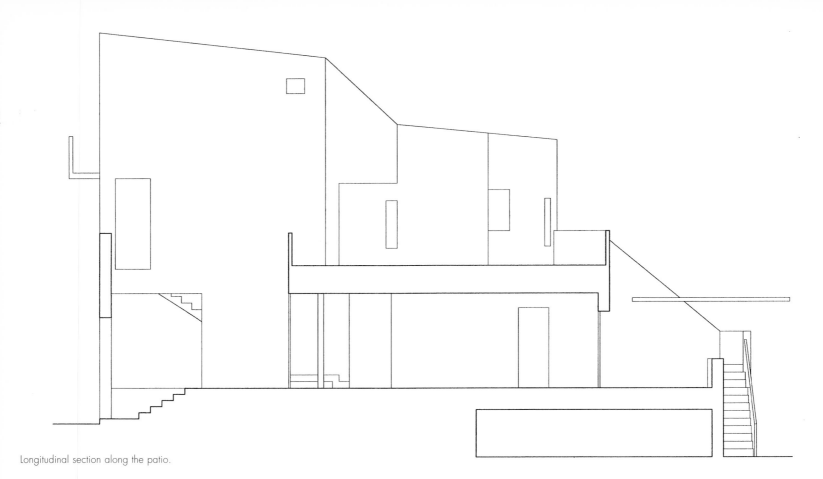

Longitudinal section along the patio.

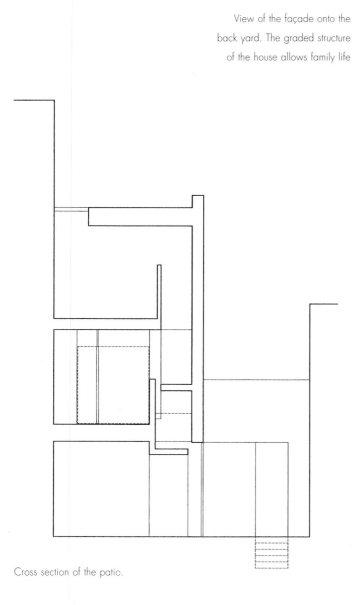

Cross section of the patio.

View of the façade onto the
back yard. The graded structure
of the house allows family life

There are two facades to the house, a public one giving on to the street and a private one giving on to the first floor terrace.

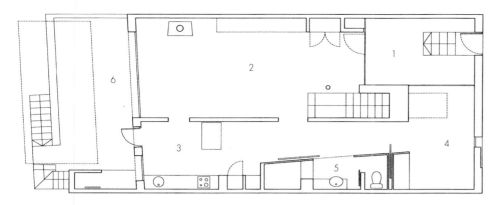

Ground floor.

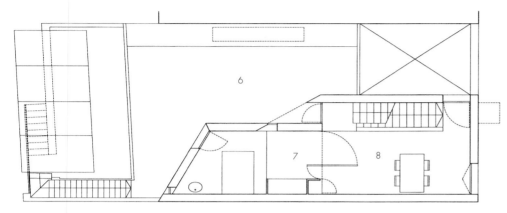

Second floor.

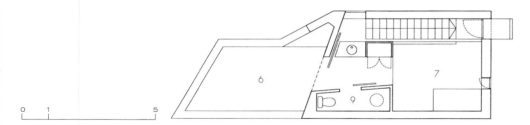

Third floor.

1. Courtyard.
2. Living room.
3. Cocina-comedor.
4. Kitchen/dining room.
5. Bathroom.
6. Terrace.
7. Bedroom.
8. Study.
9. Toilet.

0   1   5

Detail of the skylight wchich connects the living room with the first floor terrace.

Previous page,
the master bedroom and studio on the first floor.

Natural lighting varies the hue of each flight of the stairway. The architects have arranged the windows so that in ascending from the ground floor one seems to be moving toward the light.

Duffy House

Location: Sitges, Spain.

Date of construction: 1997.

Architects: Ivan Bercedo, Jorge Mestre.

Collaborators: Dominik Schleipen (equipo de diseño), Josep Maria Ambrós (arquitecto técnico), Jesús Marín (constructor), Ricardo Mayne (carpintería), Islathermic (aluminio).

Photographers: Jordi Miralles, Dominik Schleipen.

Rosenthal House

J. Frank Fitzgibbons

It is hard to believe, but this bold, sculptural family house with its intriguing geometry, located in Santa Monica, is the metamorphosis of a craftsman's cottage which originally stood on the site. When architect Frank Fitzgibbons first visited this 150-foot-long plot with his clients, the Rosenthals, with a brief to extend the cottage, it soon became clear that all they really wanted to salvage was the view. In the end only the garage was kept of the original building, along with the garden which became a central part of their project for a family home.

Tom and Susan Rosenthal were enthralled with Fitzgibbons' work on the Nottingham residence in the late eighties. Clearly the forthright modernist approach they appreciated in him would have been severely handicapped if restricted to the renovation. Particularly in view of their demanding brief: the program should include a public area for entertaining, a library, private quarters and a liberal family living area, where the inevitable chaos generated by two small children would not matter, as well as a master suite that must be oriented towards Santa Monica's renowned sunsets. "At the same time, they also wanted an open California feeling', comments the architect. So it was a happy day when demolition was decided upon.

Fitzgibbons' solutions have created a house with a strong contemporary feel, loosely L-shaped. The short stroke of the "L" has been tweaked slightly so that its first-floor axis is rotated to the street and its upper-level axis is parallel to it. Being at the western edge of the plot this volume shields the garden from the street and provides shade when the Californian sun is at its hottest. This part "fronts" the house, incorporating the more sophisticated public area, while the long stroke is devoted to family. This rear wing is set back as far as possible against the northern limit of the property to maximise the garden area, a priority for the clients. The first-floor rooms all have access to the garden and apart from the master bedroom, looking west, all the rooms focus on the garden as the heart of the composition.

The quite austere forms with blocks of colour as surface are reminiscent of Le Corbusier. It differentiates from the early moderns in plan though: the abstract twisting of the two geometries as a reference to the geometry of the site is a device used by contemporary architects to make the project tie in at a conceptual level with its surroundings. This superimposition of geometry then allows the incorporation of balconies, overhangs and so on to be established within the framework of the house. The composition of interior and exterior surfaces comes from the collision between geometries. The house is restrained though and uses a contemporary minimalist language for the resolution of some of the details.

Approaching from the street, a flight of stairs covers the 22-foot-slope from street level to entry level. The plan of the house can be seen from the front door— living and dining room on either side, the stair tower ahead and an open sight line through the length of the property. The library is like a gallery on the upper floor, open to the living room below. The lime, green stair tower is the hinge of the house, where the two volumes intersect. According to the architect, "the summation of the geometry occurs here". The family rooms in the rear wing include children's bedrooms with their own balcony jutting over a terrace into the garden, and a guest suite.

Whether it is Fitzgibbons' experience as painter and sculptor, or the influence of the masters of color in modern architecture in neighbouring Mexico that affects the way he uses it, there is no doubt that color plays an important role in his work. Here the blocks of unusual colors and variations of stucco texture strengthen the expression of the two axes. Indoors, too, color is used to articulate junctions and add warm tones to the white expanse, which is also broken up by sculptural details like nooks and crannies in the double-height living room wall. There is little doubt that in this dazzling Californian home both artist and architect have been at work and left their mark —with a most impressive result.

The house is divided into public and private areas on the ground floor which all have access to the garden. The staircase provides a focal point for the entrance sequence and the pivot linking the two wings of the house. The master bedroom looks back over the entrance to the views whilst the other rooms focus on the garden as the heart of the composition and the house itself.

As a painter, sculptor and architect Frank Fitzgibbons uses color, texture and form in fascinating ways. Commenting on the stair tower he says, "as it interlaces the major axes, tying them together, its aubergine color etches its way about the separate legs of the L acknowledging their interdependency. This is an idea that has fascinated me in the work of Christo's rope and fabric wrappings of various buildings, and Dievenkorn's line versus color field paintings in his Ocean Park series".

Full of interesting designer
pieces of modern furniture, the
house's open spaces and
simplicity make it a perfect
showcase for anything from
Noguchi to Jacobsen.

Ground floor plan.

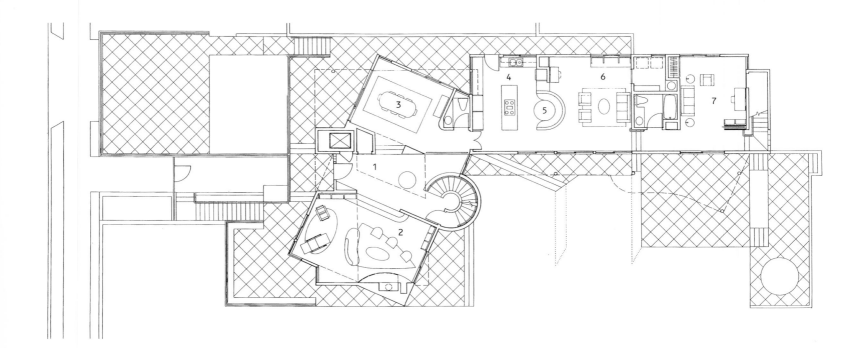

First floor plan.

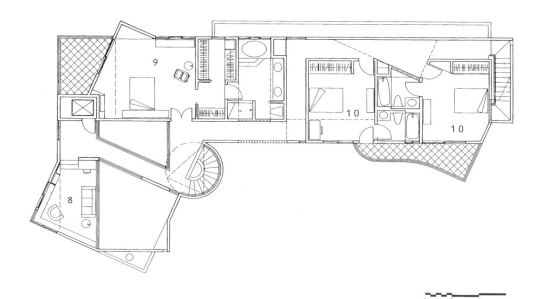

0   5   10   15

Rosenthal House

Location: Santa Monica, California, USA.

Completion date: 1996.

Architect: J. Frank Fitzgibbons.

Collaborators: Gimmy Tranquillo (design), Niver Engineering (structure), G.M. Construction (constructor).

Photographer: Toshi Yoshimi.

Schöener House

Grupo LBC

This house is one of a group of three which share the same access road and are all surrounded by a single wall made of volcanic rock. The terrain is on a fairly sharp incline which descends from west to east, or from the back of the house to the entrance. The lot is virtually rectangular and measures approximately 50 by 130 feet. The house has no view: it is surrounded by the neighboring houses and the private access road.

An asphalt patio, 16 feet wide by 40 long, lies behind the stone wall, serving as an open-air garage. This is a space which is meant to be passed through quickly: just enough time to leave the car and enter the house. The stairs leading to the main entrance are located in a corner, near the pedestrian access.

If the garage is considered part of the private space of a house, then it can be said that the residence takes up the whole lot. Under this perspective, what is unique about this house is that it has no real façade, since the rooms are all set flush against the surrounding wall. Because of this, the only façade the house has is the other side of the wall, which surrounds the gardens of the neighboring houses. The side of the house that faces out onto the outdoor garage has only a few small service windows corresponding to the kitchen and laundry rooms.

The project is therefore completely introspective: it completely ignores its surroundings. Although it is located on a slope, almost the entire building consists of one ground floor, which is 115 feet deep and elevated 6 feet above the point of access. All of these characteristics derive from one initial decision that defines the entire project: to build the house around a patio.

In contrast to its hermetic attitude towards the exterior, the inside of the house is spacious and open, with lines of sight that extend as far as 65 feet. The house is arranged in three bands which run perpendicular to the party walls. The first band houses the social area: the community spaces of the house. The living room, kitchen and other services are on the ground floor, with a smaller living room on the second floor. The patio takes up the 40-foot wide central band. The designers of this part of the house, López Baz and Alfonso Calleja, combine paved surfaces with plant and flower beds, as well as a pond raised 3 feet above the ground. The third band, at the back of the house, holds the bedrooms with their respective bathrooms.

Like the Celaya house dealt with in the next chapter, which was also built by LBC, this residence displays a clear separation between the common or public areas and the private rooms. The patio is the central nucleus of the house and serves as a common outdoor meeting place, while at the same time dividing it into two parts and putting distance between them. The bedrooms are a 55-yard walk from the steps at the entrance of the house. Nevertheless, the halls and corridors are not bland, faceless spaces. Each one is unique: one, for example, has a large window looking out onto the patio, while another is lit from overhead by a vaulted skylight.

The architects have provided each room with its own unique look and atmosphere. In this way, the house can respond to the various uses, needs and situations that can arise in any home.

Schöener House

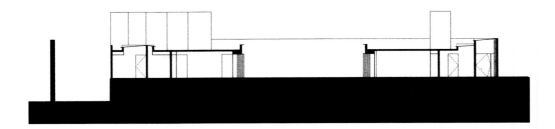

Longitudinal section.

View of the entrance with the party wall made of volcanic rock in the foreground.

1. Entrance walkway.
2. Entrance road.
3. Garage.
4. Vestibule.
5. Fireplace.
6. Living room.
7. Toilet.
8. Washing and ironing room.
9. Kitchen.
10. Terrace.
11. Pond.
12. Garden.
13. Passageway.
14. Main bedroom.
15. Main bathroom.
16. Bedroom.
17. Bathroom.

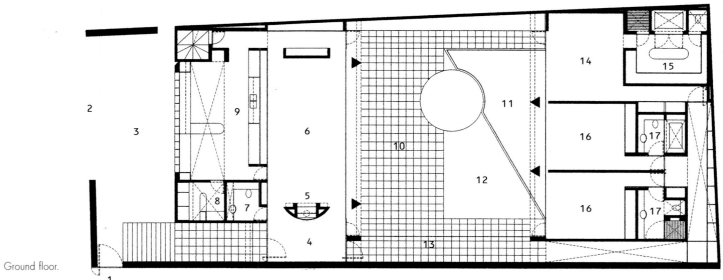

Ground floor.

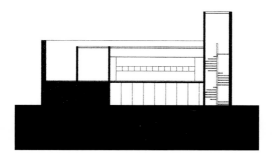

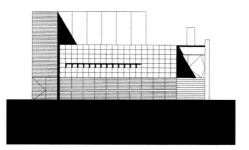

Cross section.

Elevation of the entrance.

One of the most characteristic elements of this house is the huge steel porticoes at both ends of the patio. The base of the pillars is an equilateral triangle with one of its vertices pointing towards the patio. The dark color of the metal porticoes was obtained through the natural rusting of the steel, which was later treated with an impermeable sealant to protect it. Half of the pilasters are submerged in a large metal tank.

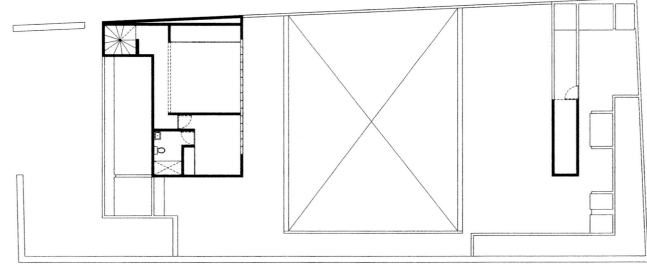

Planta primera.

The pavement is mainly composed of wood and travertine marble.

The fireplace acts as a separating element between the living room and the area leading from the entrance to the corridor that crosses the patio.

Schöener House

Location: El Pedregal de San Ángel, México.

Date of construction: 1993.

Architects: Alfonso López Baz, Javier Calleja Ariño.

Collaborators: Raúl Pulido, Octavio Cardoza.

Photographs: Fernando Cordero.

use Schöener House
chöener House
House Schöener House
öener House
er House Schöener
ouse Schöener House
er House Schöener House
öener House Schöener
ener House Schöener
a Schöener
ner House Schöener

House in Bosques de Las Lomas

Gutiérrez Cortina Arquitectos

While the recovery of local architectural styles and traditional building techniques is a commendable trend, the results are more often than not merely trivial, picturesque exercises in kitsch. As a result, works of this type often look dated just a few years after their construction. Nevertheless, popular architecture is anything but trivial, and is based on solid, rational construction principles, economical materials and simple, austere decoration. As Le Corbusier admitted, there is no better way to build a modern structure than by going back to tradition. The desire to regain the simplicity of popular architecture is evident throughout his work.

However, this equating of the modernity with tradition is prevalent in few parts of the world. One of them is Mexico. Starting with Luis Barragán, Mexican architecture has a style of its own that preserves the best characteristics of traditional rural architecture, giving priority to the essential aspects while avoiding the merely trivial or picturesque. This movement combines careful attention to lighting with uncompromising design, and preserves many of the characteristics of the traditional Mexican haciendas and country houses, such as open-air patios with ponds, intense colors, roughly textured walls and solid wood furniture.

It must be pointed out, however, that while this approach works well on a domestic scale, it is less successful in urban settings. Many of the admirable characteristics of the architecture of Barragán — and later in Mathias Goeritz, Ricardo Legorreta, Katy Horna, Montiel Blancas and Gutiérrez Cortina — make sense in the calm, spacious atmosphere of a country house, but are not at all appropriate for noisy, crowded cities.

For this reason, the most interesting and attractive works in Mexican architecture are found in the country, or in the residential suburbs of Mexico City: El Pedregal de San Angel, Bosques de la Herredura, or in this case, Bosques de Las Lomas.

The house is located on a walled-in lot measuring 19 yards wide by 38 deep. The last 11 yards at the back of the lot comprise to the backyard. The lot has a considerable slope: the back is 10 yards higher than the street level at the front. This allows the house to be conceived as a series of graded terraces.

The residence is arranged around three private patios, each surrounded by walls. The front patio is actually a terrace which covers the garage, while the back one is a private patio connected to the master bedroom and the second-floor family room. The third, located in the center of the house, is covered by a pergola and glass plating and partly closed in by a slab of concrete. Domestic life revolves around this central patio, which is accessible by means of a staircase that ascends from the entrance to the main floor of the house. This staircase functions as a large atrium which connects the different areas of the residence.

The main floor holds the community spaces of the house: the living room-dining room, which opens out onto both the front patio and the atrium, and the library. The service areas are also located on this floor: the kitchen and service room as well as a laundry room and an area for hanging out clothes.

The second floor is occupied by the bedrooms and a family living room. Because of the slope of the terrain, these rooms allow direct access to the back yard without having to go upstairs.

House in Bosques de Las Lomas

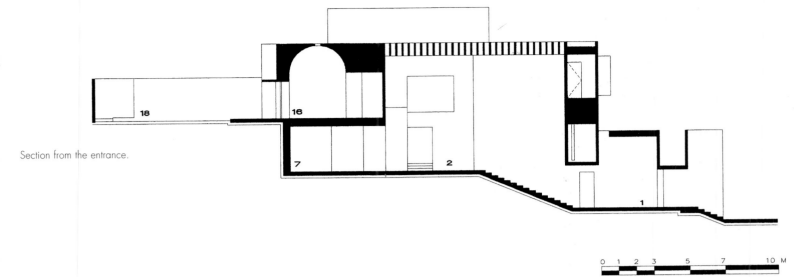

Section from the entrance.

18   16   7   2   1

0 1 2 3   5   7   10 M

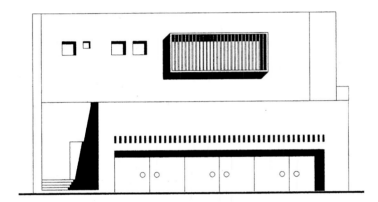

Street façade.

"It is difficult to explain the principles that motivate us, but I can say that a great deal of it has to do with the emotions we feel when we move around in the spaces that we have imagined. This is why we identify with our popular architecture and all its authentic derivations." Bosco Gutiérrez Cortina

On the following page, a panoramic view of the atrium.

68

Many of the techniques
employed seek to create a
visual effect. The stairway
which leads from the entrance
to the atrium becomes
gradually narrower as it goes
up. As a result, only the
overhead pergola of the atrium
is visible from the entrance,
along with a bare, blue-
colored tube surrounded by
crimson walls.

Main floor

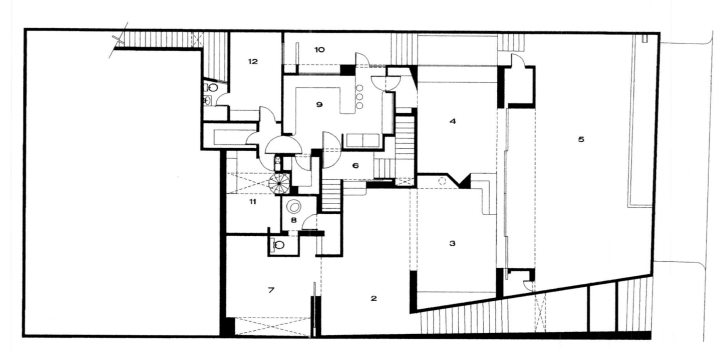

1. Entrance.
2. Interior patio.
3. Room.
4. Dining room.
5. Exterior patio
6. Vestibule.

7. Library.
8. Bathroom.
9. Kitchen.
10. Service patio.
11. Laundry room.
12. Service room.

13. Master bedroom.
14. Children's bedroom.
15. Girl's bedroom.
16. Family room.
17. Dressing room.
18. Garden.

Second floor.

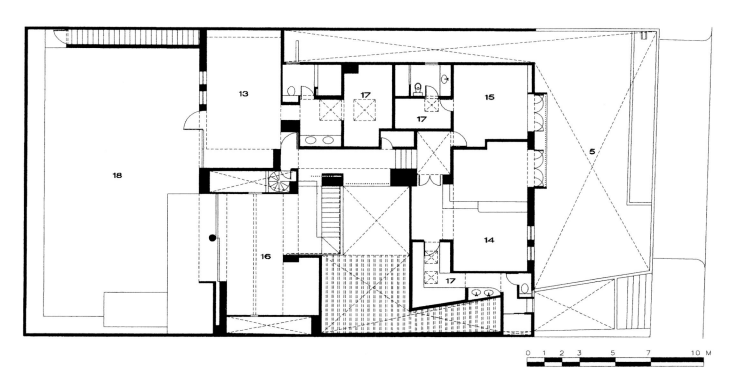

0 1 2 3   5   7   10 M

House in Bosques de Las Lomas

Location: Bosque de Las Lomas, Mexico City.

Date of construction: 1995.

Architects: Bosco Gutiérrez Cortina, Fernando Cárdenas González, Emilio Guerrero y Ramos, Alejandro Medina Macías.

Collaborator: Roberto Stark (structure).

Photographers: Alberto Moreno Guzmán.

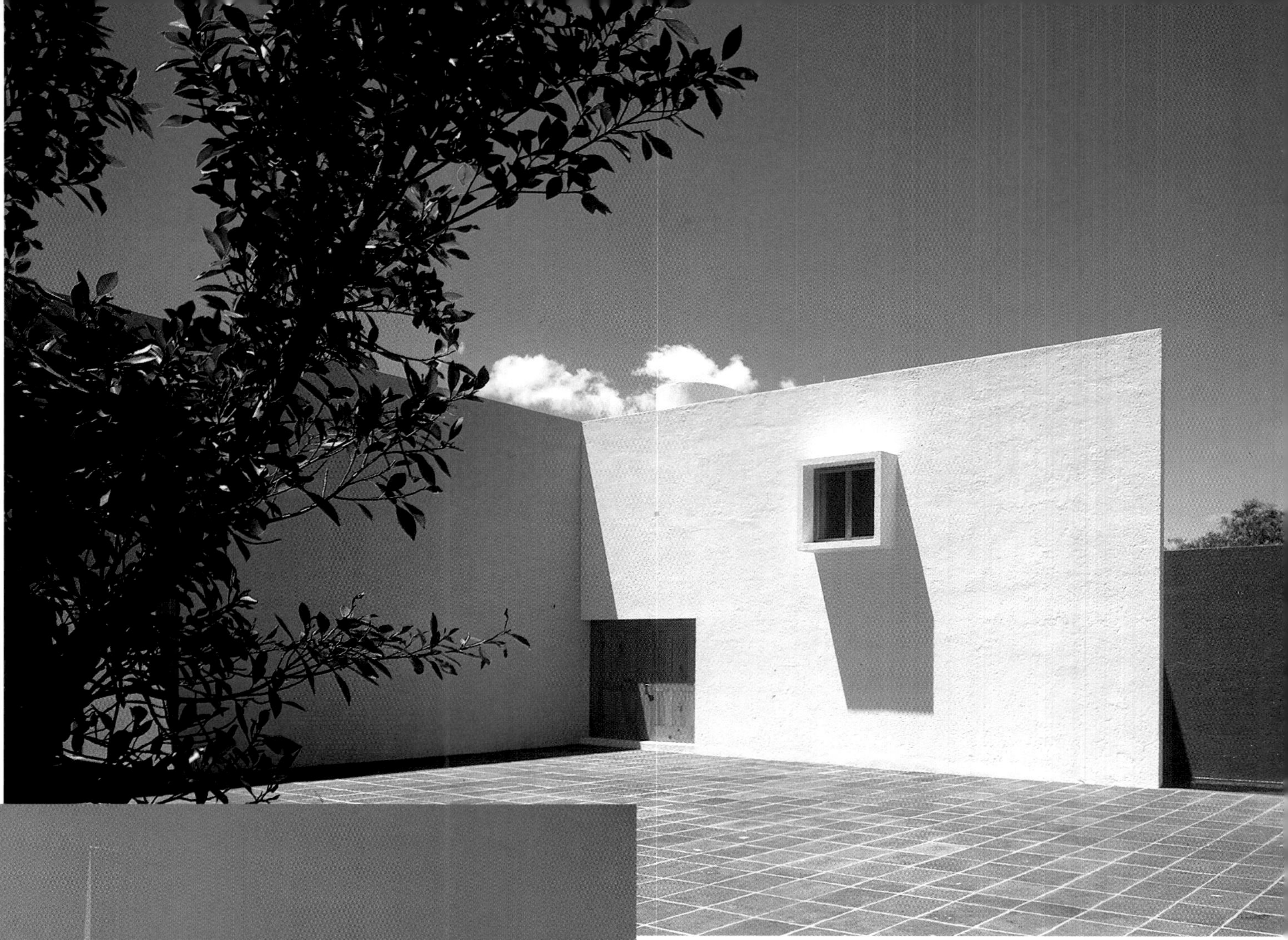

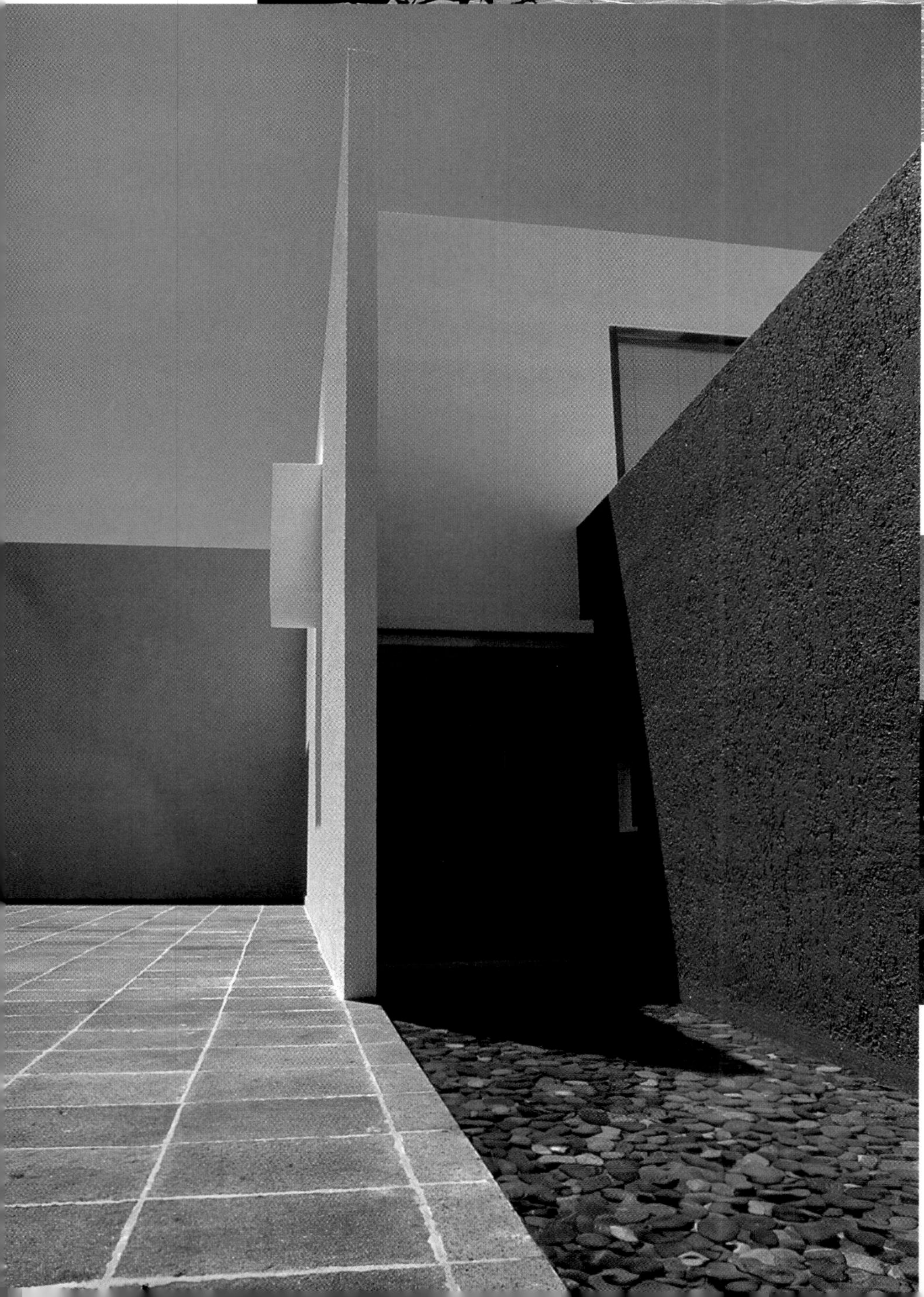

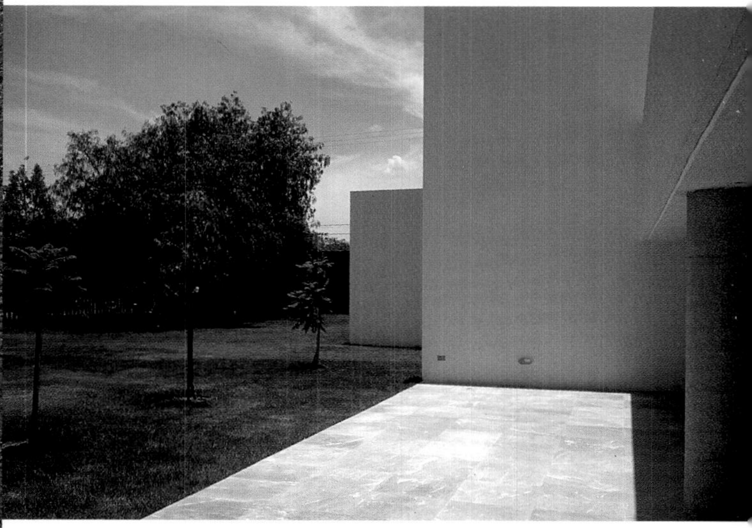

House in Querétaro

Gutiérrez Cortina Arquitectos

"Besides being functional, architectural form must be beautiful and have sculptural qualities. As a result, the simpler a design is, the more clarity, impact and emotional resonance it has." Bosco Gutiérrez Cortina.

Although his architecture is often seen as an attempt to recover local architectural traditions, in our opinion Gutiérrez Cortina's work belongs to one of the twentieth century's greatest currents: abstractionism. His concern for geometric composition, with perfectly defined planes and clear volumes has much in common with the works of Rietveld, Mondrian, Barnett Newman, Sol Lewitt, or Frank Stella. Like all of these architects, Gutiérrez Cortina seeks harmony through geometric and chromatic combinations, and he is convinced that abstraction in itself is enough to stir the senses and arouse emotions.

As Gutiérrez Cortina admits in the preceding quotation, the initial phases of his architectural design take a clearly sculptural, or formalist, approach. It is not enough for a building to be functional and comfortable, with correct distribution of space; it should also be conceived as a work of art. Gutiérrez Cortina's concern with tradition is an additional quality, not the crux of his architectural style.

This house is located on the outskirts of Querétaro, in a residential area near a golf course. The lot borders on the golf course on one side, and on a dividing wall on another. The other sides are limited by two streets that cross each other at one of the vertices of the lot. The plot is completely flat and measures 33 yards wide by 55 deep, making a total area of 16,146 square feet.

The architect takes advantage of these characteristics in two ways: by building the house almost entirely on one level, and by designing a large, square plaza at the front of the house. This plaza acts as an anteroom to the house, and although it belongs to the same property, it is conceived as a space which is separate from the house itself. The technique of placing the house some distance back from the street is often employed in public architecture in order to leave enough space in the crowded urban surroundings for the building to be easily seen and appreciated. It can also be used occasionally for guest parking.

The main façade has virtually no openings: only two doors, (one for the house and one for the garage) and one window for the study. The lack of doors and windows gives the façade an imposing, monumental look. The silent, blind walls that surround the paved plaza contribute to the quiet, empty feeling of the place.

The residence is divided into two clearly separate areas: one for common or public use (living room, dining room, kitchen and bathrooms) and another private area, with three large bedrooms and a small sitting room.

On the floor plan, the two areas form two squares which are connected at their vertices. The entrance to the house is located precisely at this point. The vestibule is cut in half by a wedge-shaped volume containing the staircase which leads to the study, which is the only room on the second floor.

Facing the entrance is a huge, two-story window which affords a breathtaking view of the garden and the golf course. This panorama creates a marked contrast with the hermetic façade. To reach the living room, a visitor must go around the wedge-shaped wall and down a few steps. In this way the vestibule creates a barrier between daytime and evening activities, with a separate area dedicated to each. As in other of Gutiérrez Cortina's projects, there is an effort to put a distance between the different areas of the house, so that a change of activity implies a clear change of place.

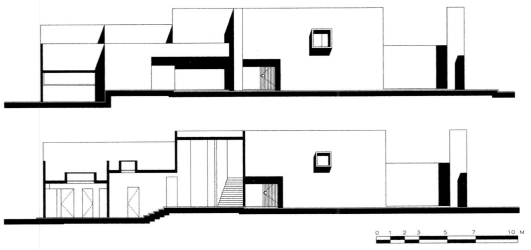

Transversals sections.

In the "private" area of the house, a small pond and a cobalt blue wall face the family sitting room.

The construction of the house on one floor permits the use of skylights to light the inner bedrooms and the service rooms, as can be seen in this section.

On the next page, various details of the main vestibule and the large window that looks out onto the garden. The cross-shaped carpentry is inspired by one of the windows of Luis Barragan's house in Tacubaya.

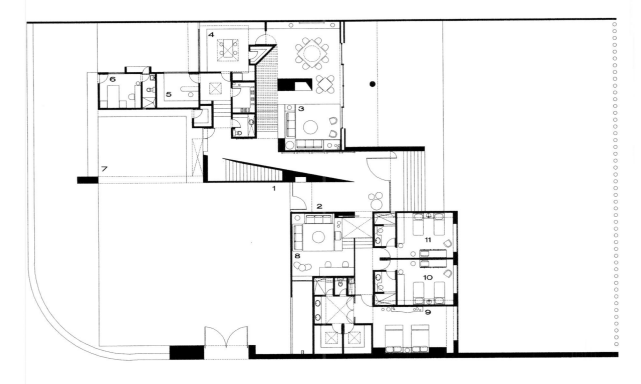

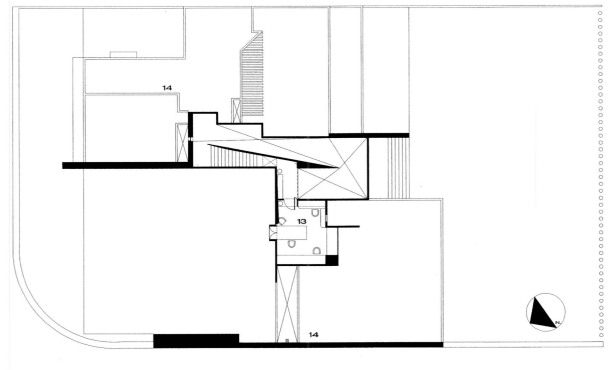

Various details of the living room.
As in the house in Bosque de Las
Lomas, the fireplace is used to
separate the living room from
the dining room.

House in Querétaro

Location: Querétaro, Mexico.

Completion date: 1997.

Architects: Bosco Gutiérrez Cortina, Fernando Cárdenas González, Emilio Guerrero y Ramos, Alejandro Medina Macías.

Collaborators: Roberto Stark (structures).

Photographer: Alberto Moreno Guzmán.

Stampfel House

Wolfgang Döring

The Döring & Partners architectural firm was contracted to construct six houses in a new residential area near Düsseldorf. Almost all of the clients were contemporary art collectors or owners of art galleries. Both Stampfel House and the project dealt with in the next chapter, Bielicky House, are part of this recently completed group of houses.

The influence of Walter Gropius, Marcel Breuer, and Bruno Taut, all masters of the German Modern Movement, is apparent in both houses. Some of the principal features of this influence are the rigorous application of geometry, the finishings, and the use of hollow spaces.

This house, however, is laid out in an almost perfectly symmetrical fashion, which is rarely found in modern architecture, and has more in common with the Beaux Arts tradition. Nevertheless, symmetry is not used here as a method of composition or method of constructing a balanced and attractive façade, but rather as a way of arranging and organizing space in the simplest and most direct way possible.

Careful examination of the floor plans and sections of the house reveals that it would be difficult to lay out a house with double-height rooms, interior patios, and metallic footbridges in a simpler way. The two-story plan is perfectly rectangular and divided in half by a longitudinal wall that supports the staircase in the center. The spaces intended for common use (living room, dining room and patio) are located in the wider bay. The narrow bay holds the private and service rooms (bedrooms, kitchen, bathrooms, and sauna). The spaces that are meant to be accessible to visitors and guests are located on the ground floor, whereas the rooms intended for use by the owners are upstairs. The garage is housed in a separate building, as is the machinery needed for the heating and plumbing of the house.

Faced with the sheer simplicity and practicality of its arrangement, a much richer insight into the building can be gained by looking at specific aspects of the project. It is here that the magic lying behind the structure becomes apparent.

Two examples of this are the Japanese fish pond (koi) and the garden with abstract pillars and rows of trees, both located near the house. These are not conceived as exterior spaces, but rather as an extension of the house itself. The pond is an exact continuation of the bay that holds the living room. In fact, the large windows on both sides of the house afford a complete view of the entire plot, from the garage to the wall at the end. The reflections in the pond create an inverted image of the double-height spaces over the dining room and the entrance, as well as the terrace which is hidden on the second floor.

There is no front hall for receiving guests inside the house, since this function is provided on the outside by the space between the garden gate and the front door. The footbridges that cross the double spaces are intended only to access the small balconies on both of the side façades. The fence that surrounds the house shields the inside from sight. Only vague blotches of color can be seen from the street as the light shines through the translucent glass of the second-floor patio.

Döring's austere and geometrical concept of architecture strives to bring to the foreground aspects which are too often hidden by an accumulation of spectacular images and effects.

Stampfel House

Site plan.

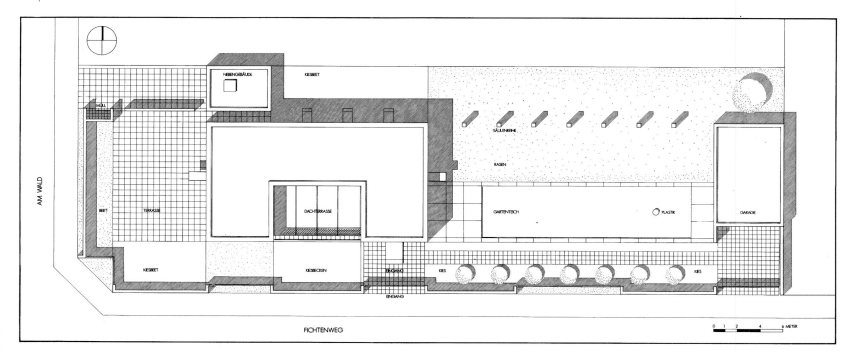

The garden was designed by Bernhard Korte. The Japanese fish pond, the side façade of the house, the wall of the garage, and the row of concrete pillars outline a perfectly rectangular shape. There is no grass in the garden, the ground is mostly covered with gravel.

Elevations.

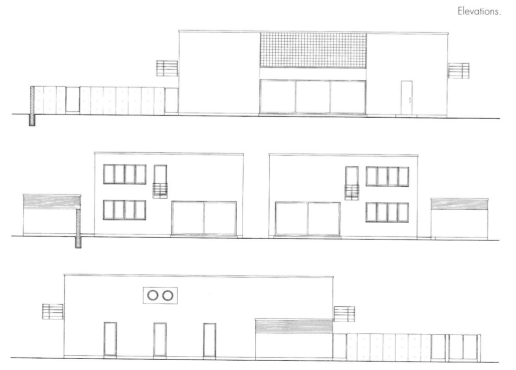

Ground floor.

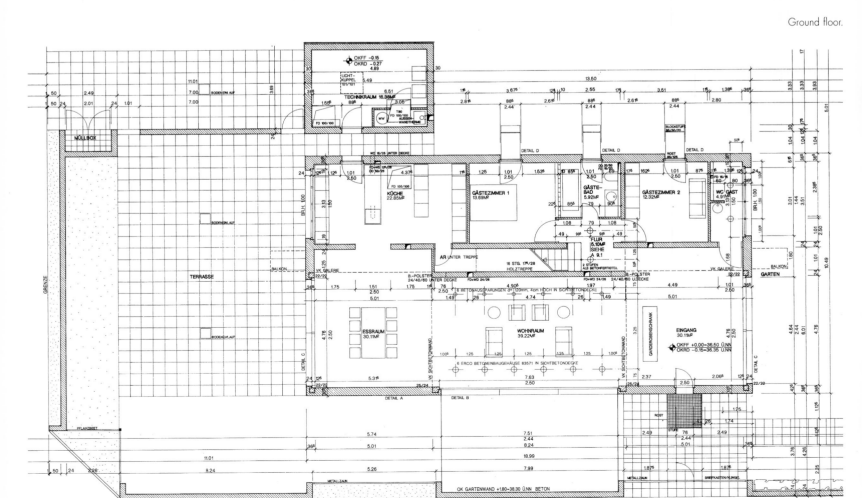

Although the Stampfel house has a surface area of almost 3,000 square feet, it was built for just two people. The load-bearing walls are made of special concrete blocks. These blocks have an exceptional capacity for retaining heat, which is especially important in Germany, where people give great importance to energy conservation.

Longitudinal section.

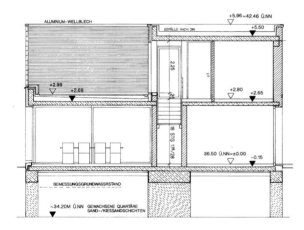

Modern art paintings from the owners' collection hang from almost all of the walls of the house.

General view and details of the
bathroom on the second floor.

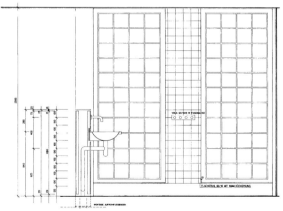

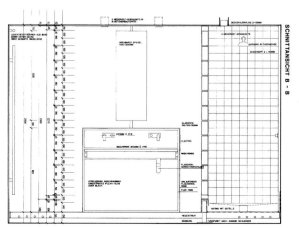

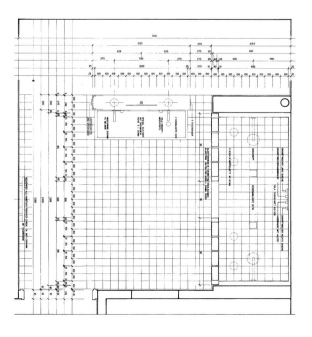

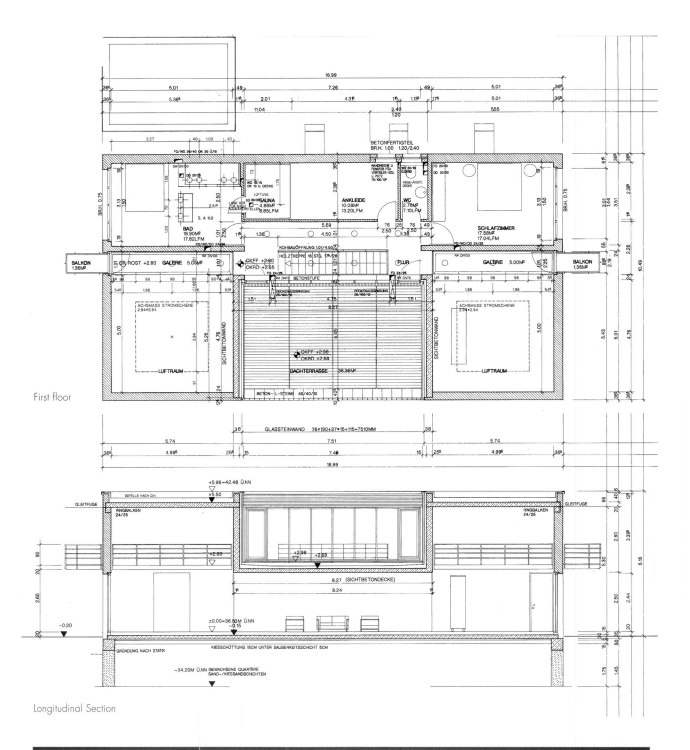

First floor

Longitudinal Section

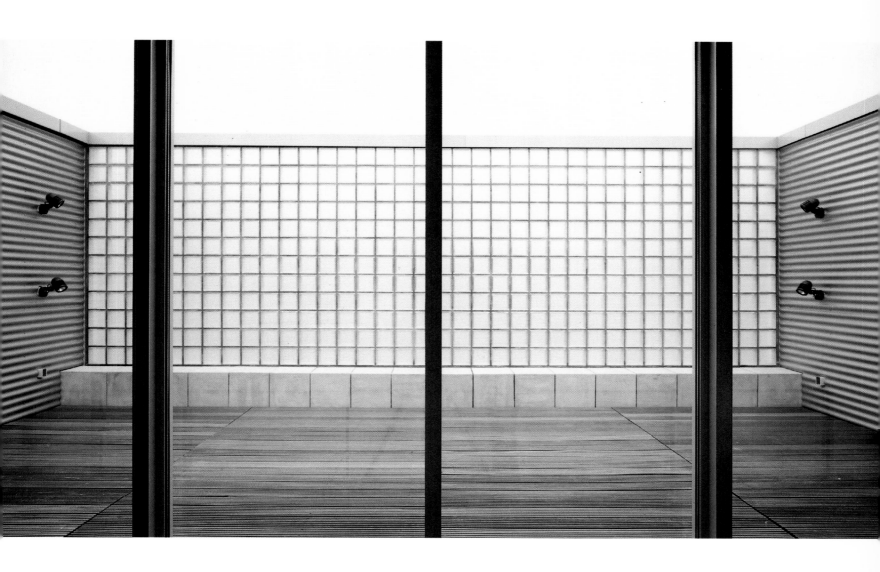

Stampfel House

Location: Düsseldorf, Germany

Date of construction: 1995

Architect: Wolfgang Döring

Collaborators: Bernhard Korte

Photographers: Dieter Leistner, Frank Springer

Bielicky House

Wolfgang Döring

This house is located in the lot next to the Stampfel house. It was constructed at approximately the same time, and the similarities between the two are apparent. A comparison of the two allows us to confirm certain ideas, dispel doubts and analyze concepts in more depth.

Once again, the style employed is austere and unadorned, with details that are inspired by the modern tradition: metallic-tube railings, narrow balconies, sliding windows, and white walls. The exterior volume of the building is again a perfect prism: nothing protrudes from the flat surfaces of the façades.

Unlike the Stampfel house, there is no symmetry in its arrangement, although the methods used in organizing the spaces in the two houses are surprisingly similar. A wall cuts lengthwise through the house, acting as a point of connection. This wall supports the staircase and separates the smaller rooms from the larger ones and the double-height areas. In this case the division is almost complete, since it coincides with the skylight in the roof, the stairwell and a long, narrow opening in the wrought iron over the hall.

But what is especially interesting about this house is Döring's treatment of the outer "skin" of the building. The façade facing the street is completely hermetic. On the ground floor, the doors of the house's two garages and the front entrance make up a metal strip that covers the entire façade. Similarly, a wall of translucent glass seals off the first floor. Because of the type of structure and the materials used, the front part of the house, which contains the garages, the entrance, and the first-floor terrace, could almost be considered an independent building attached to the house. In fact, the fence surrounding the house starts from this line, and there is a second entrance to the house on the other side of the corridor between the two garages. The result is that there is no single façade, but rather a series of insulating layers. The house is conceived as a shield which protects the inhabitants from the outside world.

An additional benefit of this concept is that it frees Döring from having to create an attractive or original façade for the house. As we have seen, the Bielicky house is preeminently practical and austere. The architect must have been reluctant to put a "pretty face" on the house with superfluous adornments.

The house was designed for a family of five: a couple with three children. It has one master bedroom and three for the children, all of them on the first floor. The children's bedrooms lack windows onto the street. Instead, their windows look out onto a large terrace surrounded by a wall made of translucent glass blocks.

The living room is a large, double-height space, with almost no furniture, which can be used as a concert hall. Although it is located in a corner of the building, it can be considered the real center of the house, because it forms part of a larger area which includes the paved terrace behind the large windows.

Bielicky House

View of the Stampfel and Bielicky
residences from another house
designed by Döring. As is clear from
this view, the houses do not face in
the same direction: the entrances are
perpendicular to each other.

Front elevation.

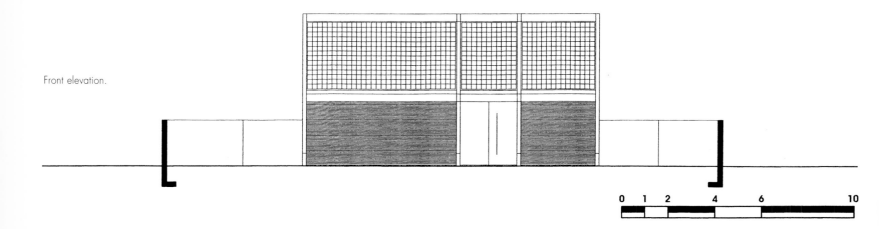

0 1 2 4 6 10

Corner detail.

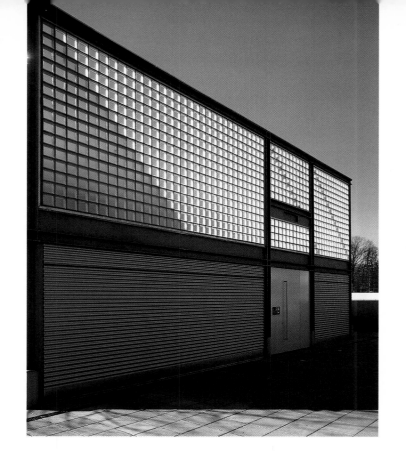

The block with a metallic structure and walls made of glass blocks and metallic sheet, houses the garages on the ground floor and a terrace on the first floor. It acts as a kind of isolation chamber which separates the private interior rooms from the street. The house actually has two entrances: one on the street façade and one at the end of the corridor that crosses the glass volume.

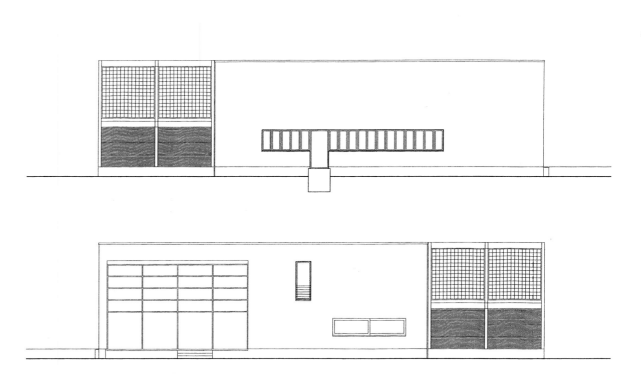

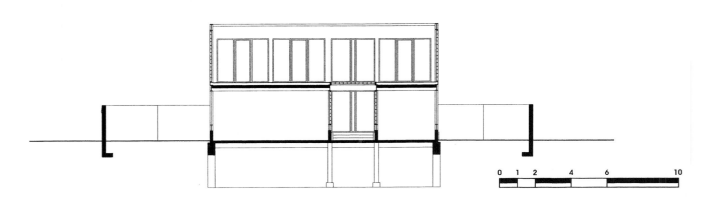

0 1 2   4   6   10

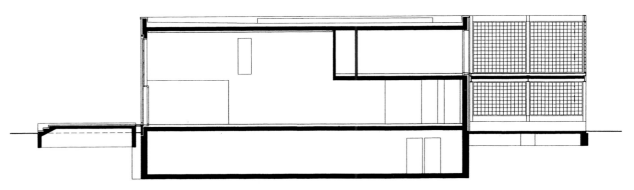

Cross section.

Besides their interest in contemporary art, the Bielicky family shares a great love of music. For this reason, the living room has been designed to function as a small concert hall. The ceiling, for instance, is made of special sound-absorbent material.

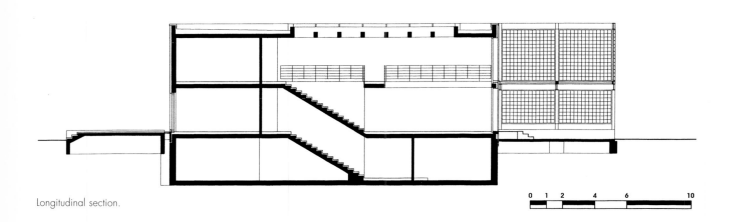

Longitudinal section.

0 1 2   4   6   10

Ground floor.

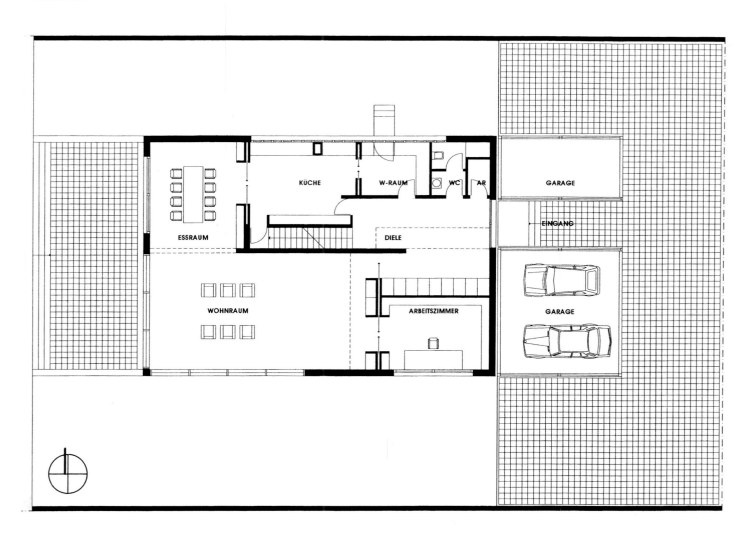

ESSRAUM   KÜCHE   W-RAUM   WC   AR   GARAGE

EINGANG

WOHNRAUM   DIELE   ARBEITSZIMMER   GARAGE

First floor.

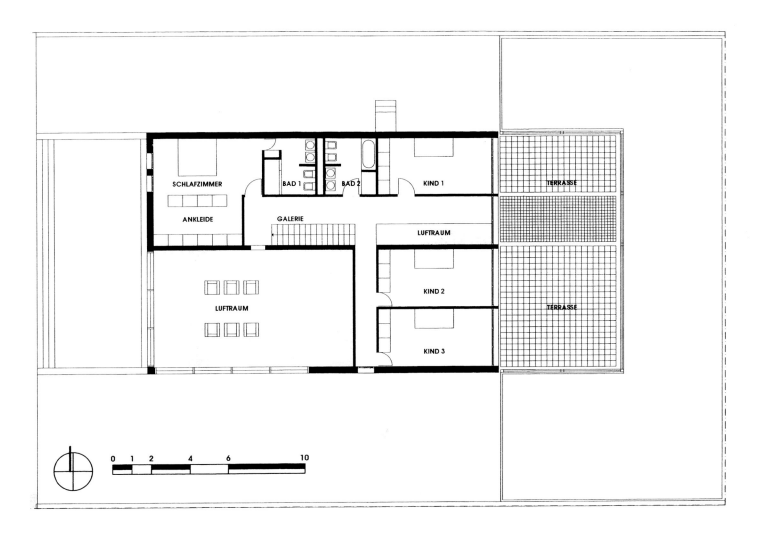

SCHLAFZIMMER

BAD 1   BAD 2

KIND 1

TERRASSE

ANKLEIDE

GALERIE

LUFTRAUM

LUFTRAUM

KIND 2

TERRASSE

KIND 3

0 1 2   4   6   10

Bielicky House

Location: Düsseldorf, Germany.

Completion date: 1995.

Architects: Wolfgang Döring, Michael Dahmen, Elmar Joeressen.

Collaborator: Georg Döring.

Photographer: Manos Meisen.

House in Na Xemena

Ramon Esteve

Na Xemena, located in the Northeast of the Mediterranean island of Ibiza, is a privileged location for any building. In this stark, rocky landscape by the sea, with cliffs that jut out into the Mediterranean, light is the dominant, enduring element. The grandeur and natural balance of this timeless panorama are awe-inspiring, and the unity of the building and its surroundings is no less so. This merging of a construction with its environment is the essence of the seductive and enduring power of great architecture.

The initial planning of the building, involving the choice of colors, materials, volumes and other elements of construction, was fluid and natural. No rigid geometrical scheme was imposed, although the design has a solid rational basis. The house is planned in such a way that it can be constantly expanded following the pattern of the original nucleus. The interior rooms have varying sizes and shapes and are added onto the main body following an upward path.

The construction climbs up the rocky base as a simple, compact whole running parallel to the shape of the cliff. From the outside, the arrangement of the terraces and the swimming pool leads the eye to the rotund shapes of the house. The whole complex strives to be a logical and unobtrusive extension of the landscape, in harmony with its surroundings. The different levels bring dynamism to the complex and delineate the outside areas such as the terraces and the swimming pool. These areas face the sea, which guarantees the unique light of the Mediterranean at all hours of the day.

The clean, basic exterior walls are perforated in order to capture the light, following a natural order determined by the interior arrangement of the rooms, with solid space predominating over the emptiness of the openings. The colors used for the exterior are obtained from natural pigments: gray for the floors and terraces and indigo for the vertical surfaces.

Three large windows made of iroco wood are embedded in the walls, framing the panorama of the terraces and swimming pool. The pool appears as a sheet of water which fuses with the sea. The interior walls, in white and cobalt blue, act as a unifying element throughout the house and are illuminated from above by the skylights.

A series of spaces leads from one to the other towards the exterior, with a sublime deference for their natural surroundings. This construction is a prime example of the importance of building with the environment instead of against it. Any setting is fragile and has a limited capacity for absorbing new images without being diluted by them. A receptive and carefully meditated consideration of the surroundings is essential in order to capture all of the implications of the topography, the sea, and the sunlight. The legitimacy that time has granted to this place can only be fully understood by prolonged contact with silence, with light and shadow, with day and night, and with land and sea.

House in Na Xemena

The entrances are protected on the outside by large metal gates in the same color as the walls. These gates close over the large windows and are integrated with the façade. At night, tiny square holes speckle the outside pavement with light.

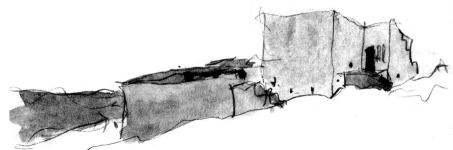

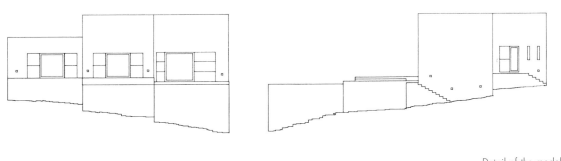

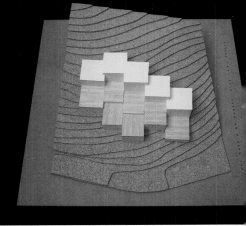

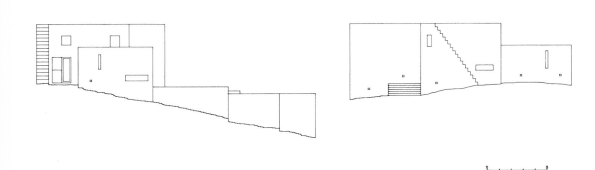

Detail of the model.

The austere geometry of the façades is completed by the stairs that give access to the house and the terraces. These climb up the terrain and outline the grounds, which are sculpted into the topography. The water of the swimming pool and benches made of old crossbeams surround the structure.

Following page: view of outside staircase during construction.

The large windows are made from a
single sheet of glass. The sliding
doors run into the walls, and the
woodwork is in iroco. All this gives
a greater sense of continuity
between the rooms and the terrace.
During the summer the windows can
be left open day and night.

Floor plan.

The program (living room, dining room, kitchen bathroom and one bedroom) was conceived as a summer house for a couple. However the modular structure allows for future extensions as well as changes in the use of each space.

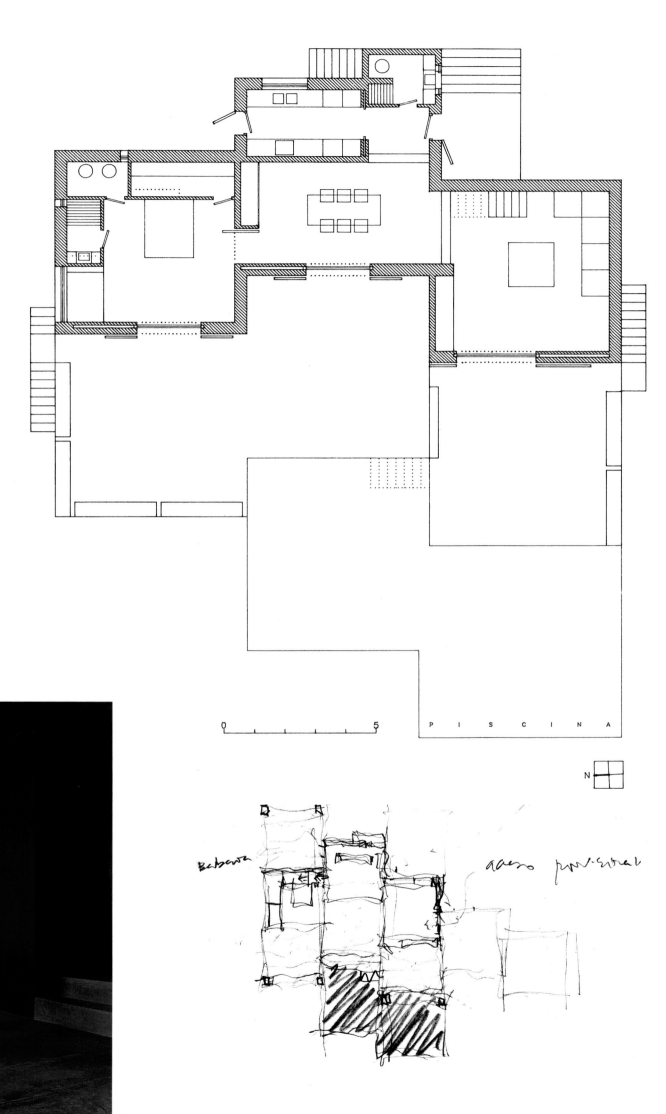

0   5

P I S C I N A

N

Bebezon   aceso provisional

Parquet made of iroco wood extends along the dining room ceiling and wall from the living room to the polished cement pavement. An interior staircase of iroco boards embedded in the wall connects the living room with the study located over the dining room. From here there is access to the upper terraces on the deck.

In the master bedroom, the bathroom facilities are clustered in one corner of the room. The sunken bathtub affords a direct view of the outside, and the iroco-wood doors are hung directly from the walls. The furnishings in the house are a direct extension of the shapes and materials used in its construction.

House in Na Xemena

Location: Ibiza, Spain.

Completion date: 1997.

Architect: Ramon Esteve.

Collaborators: Juan A. Ferrero, Antonio Calvo.

Photographer: Ramon Esteve.

Cristián Boza

Surroundings and topography always have an effect on architecture, but in some cases the relationship between the two is so profound that it is difficult to decide whether we are describing a building or a landscape. This is the case of the house at the top of a cliff near Los Vilos designed by the Chilean architect Cristián Boza. The house is so completely integrated into the surrounding terrain that it is difficult to imagine the landscape without it.

The house has an exceptional site among the rocks, facing the sea and a small island. In this area the coast comes to an abrupt stop, full of steep, jagged edges.. Small fjords, coves, craggy rocks and islets dot the seascape, forming a rich and varied visual experience. The small island protects the area from the open sea, creating a small area of calm waters, perfect for fishing, diving, or collecting shellfish.

The sun, the sea and the cliffs create a powerful and suggestive atmosphere, complete and sufficient unto itself. Visitors come to this place to observe and enjoy the landscape. Cristián Boza, although he has come to build a house, approaches it in the same way: as a spectator. He knows that any attempt to impose a new, extraneous image on this terrain is doomed to failure and would be reduced to ridicule in the face of the first sunset or rainstorm. There is no room for two perspectives in this place; the most it can accept is a whispered hint.

Boza first built a path that descends from the highest part of the property, winding its way between the rocks to the edge of the cliff in a series of terraces and graded platforms. The various rooms of the house line this narrow path. The rooms line one side of the path with the cliff on the other side. The series of doors and windows on the curved wall of this exterior corridor give the impression of a narrow village street rather than a single house. At one end of the house at the edge of the cliff, a large volume, almost nine yards high, houses the living room and dining room, as well as the master bedroom, which is located in the attic. The bedroom can be isolated from the rest of the house by means of a system of sliding wooden doors.

The roof of the house is flat and serves as an enormous terrace which is accessible from both the higher areas of the estate and the path. As Boza himself says: "this terrace is an ideal area for social life. It is over 6 yards wide by 27 long, and it ends with a system of tiered benches facing the sea, which are perfect for watching the sunset." The architect has in fact designed the house on two levels: one interior, with the rooms and another exterior, made up of the terrace, a sculptural yellow wall and the swimming pool. Access to the swimming pool is gained by crossing the wall and walking over a small metal bridge.

The different levels, itineraries and views all form part of a concept which emphasizes integration over novelty. The underlying aim is to fit the structure into an existing landscape while changing the environment as little as possible, only enough to make it into a place to eat, sleep and wait for evening while gazing at the sea from the shade of a wall. Boza's project is not innovative, but it explores the capacity of architecture to bring people closer to nature.

House in Los Vilos

The roof is level and flat, with the result that the height of the rooms increases as we proceed down the corridor/street. The highest point is the living room, which is almost nine yards high.

"The approach to landscaping strives to enhance the existing flora through the use of local creeping plants, such as pepper trees and aizoaceous shrubs, as well as cactus plants and coastal pine trees." Cristián Boza.

The Chilean architect designed the surroundings of the house with a series of landscaping elements: lookout points, stairways, pergolas, bridges and gazebos.

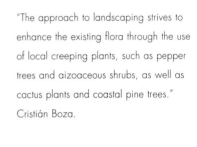

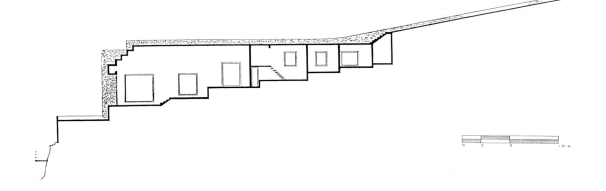

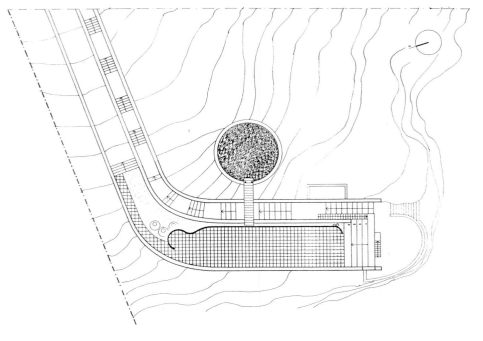

Plan of the terrace.

All of the walls are rubblework: rocks joined with cement. The interior walls are made of horizontally arranged planks of eucalyptus. The metal finishings are done in bronze.

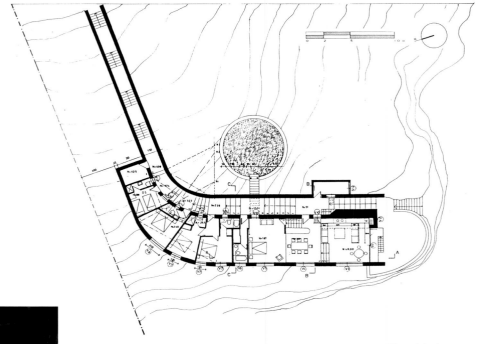

Plan of the house.

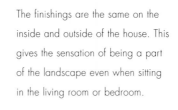

The finishings are the same on the inside and outside of the house. This gives the sensation of being a part of the landscape even when sitting in the living room or bedroom.

House in Los Vilos

Site: Los Vilos, Chile.

Completion date: 1996.

Architects: Cristián Boza.

Collaborators: Paola Durruty (project), Ricardo
Aránguiz (structures), Pablo Epulez (constructor).

Susman Bay House

Natalye Appel

Galveston Island is one of the most accessible coastal outlets for residents of Houston, Texas. To be able to escape the teeming metropolis and arrive on the shores of the Gulf of Mexico on a Friday evening sounds like every city dweller's dream. The Susman family realized that dream when they found this site located within an established home development on the west end of Galveston Island. Houston architect Natalye Appel was commissioned to construct a retreat for Steve and Karen Susman and their children, which should also be suitable for entertaining clients. Completed in 1995 the house has the immediate appeal of waterside buildings, reminiscent of boat houses and boat sheds, with the inevitable association of summer days and "messing about in boats".

However light hearted its appearance may be though, the design has fulfilled the original brief by providing generous open spaces for large gatherings, as well as private places for quiet relaxation or work. This has been achieved by what Appel describes as the "fractured bar" which forms the basis of the construction. In effect the bar is made up of two volumes clad in gray cedar clapboard, one larger and rectangular, and the other set apart; they are linked by a large "porch". Apart from providing the main entrance to the house, it bears little resemblance to conventional porches being on a much larger scale and having a different purpose. Double-height and glazed, it functions as the public space, comprising living and dining room. The other two more enclosed volumes house the private and functional elements such as bedrooms, kitchen, study and bar. The smaller one has the guest suite, making it independent from the rest of the family. These more solid buildings act like a subdued but secure backdrop to the rather flamboyant protagonist porch, with its luminosity, extravagant space and direct contact with the water. The "fracture" in the bar makes this area into a portal and directs the entry sequence towards the magnificent views across the bay.

The house has been lifted on a series of columns, allowing the ground to pass below in a technique used by the modern masters. The ground floor becomes a forest of columns providing shade and shelter, through which there are tantalizing glimpses of the water beyond. It is reminiscent of Caribbean architecture where the living area is open to the elements and the extent of the building is defined by the ground surface and the shading by the upper parts. In a similar vein a boardwalk leads from the first floor to the boat dock, where a brightly striped awning shades a terrace overlooking the inlet of Galveston Bay. Being raised above the ground enhances the views through the double-height windows of the porch. By comparison tiny windows in the rear wall guard the more private areas and encourage the eye to the front where a surprising variety of windows look over the bay.

Other details in this inner space: the gray clapboard is repeated, an inner balcony belonging to the guest room has a railing across it like the exterior windows, the same small windows as in the rear wall are featured and so on. It emphasises the idea of being in a porch attached to a house. However, being inside it reminds one of a stage set: again, the drama is in this space, exposed on this "stage", while behind the scenes a more private life goes on. Overall there is a strong sense of being outside, which, with its direct access to the water and expansive views, is what this "House as a Porch" is all about.

Raised off the ground with clapboard siding, dashes of colour, shed roofs, boardwalk and adjoining dock, the house has all the appeal of waterfront buildings associated with leisure time and vacations. The different sized windows, openings and screens reinforce this light hearted feel.

As there is a lake on the grounds, there is no swimming pool apart from an installation for small children. The house has access to pier, over which a wooden pergola has been built.

Site plan.

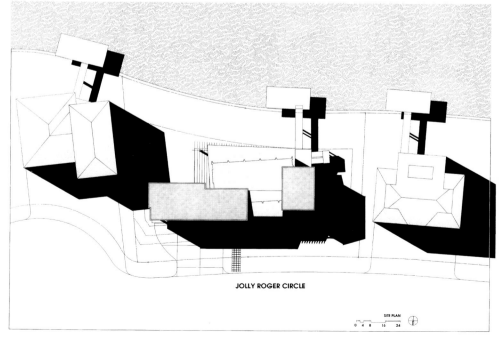

JOLLY ROGER CIRCLE

SITE PLAN

0 4 8   16   24

WATERFRONT ELEVATION

0 2 4   8   12

Bay-side facade.

Street-side facade

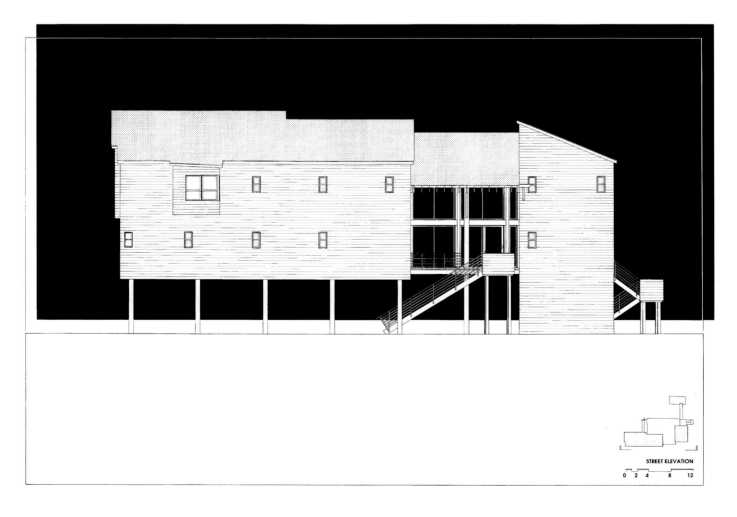

STREET ELEVATION

0   2   4   8   12

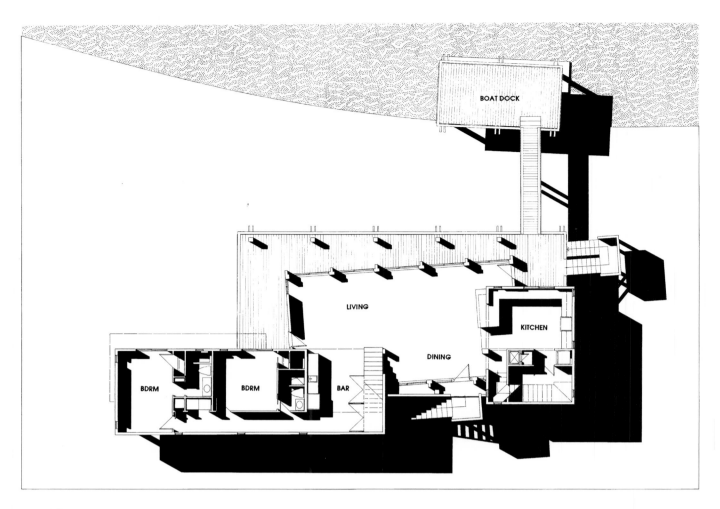

Second floor.

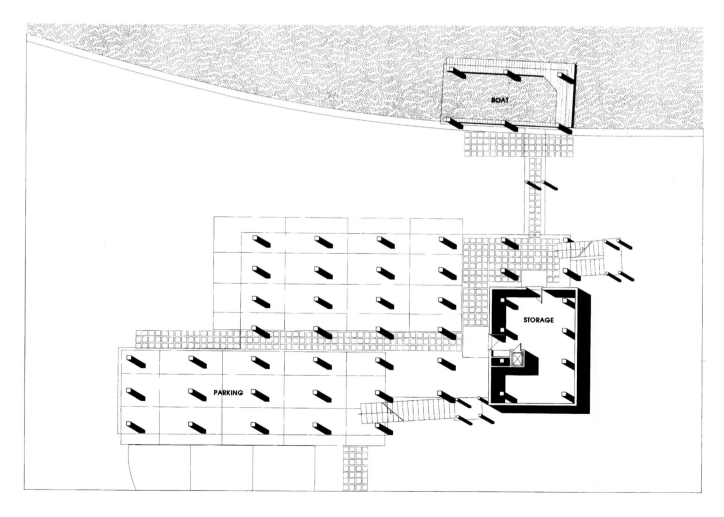

Ground floor.

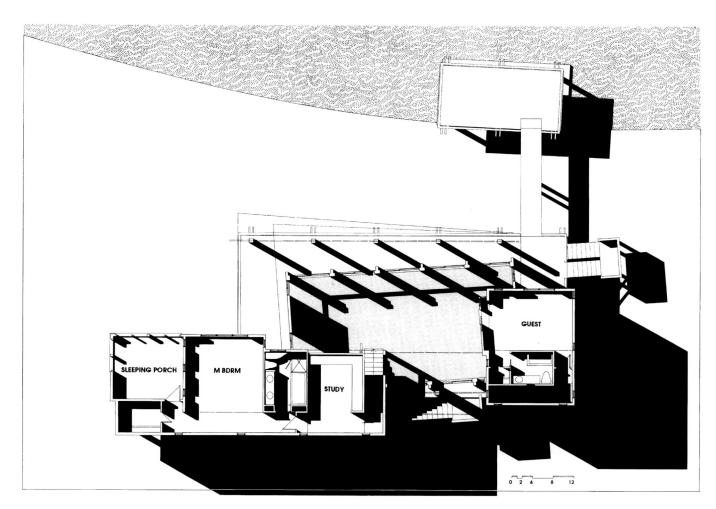

SLEEPING PORCH · M BDRM · STUDY · GUEST

0 2 4 8 12

Third floor.

LONGITUDINAL SECTION
0 2 4 8 12

Longitudinal section.

View of the central hall, lit by
hanging halogen lamps. The
air conditioning tube has also
been left exposed.

Susman Bay House

Location: Galveston, Texas, Estados Unidos.

Date of construction: 1995.

Architect: Natalye Appel.

Collaborators: Matrix Structural Engineers,

Peter J. Hurley (structure), Philip J. Douglas,

Inc. (constructor).

Photographer: Undine Pröhl.

Capistrano Beach House

Rob Wellington Quigley

The elongated plot is on a narrow strip of land, merging with the sand to the west, and with a backdrop of high, windswept cliffs to the east. This context is mirrored in the design and in the materials used: the east/west-oriented architectural planes reinforce the rigid, parallel property lines while the north/south elements are more evocative of the surrounding natural forces, the effect of the sea and the wind on the shore and cliffs echoed in gentle curves and eroded, sculptural shapes.

This 3,700 square-foot house has all the apparent glamour of the Californian Dream: large expanses of glass looking over the Pacific Ocean, wooden decks jutting into the dazzling white sand, shady upper decks to enjoy the sea breezes in privacy, a virgin beach for early morning exercise. But under the sound guidance of Rob Quigley, with the "remarkable energy and ethicality that make him the signal architect he is today", there is no chance of it falling into such a clichéd category.

Quigley's designs have always been true to the reality they are in contextually, culturally and climatically. The dramatic and exciting contrasts between the ocean and the land are interpreted architecturally: thick walls of poured concrete set off glass pavilions; deep shade and dappled light as against the dazzling glare of the sand; exposed, extrovert decks and terraces as opposed to quiet, private areas.

Circulation through the house is also full of contrasts in both the interior and exterior. Entrance on the east side is through two iron gates which lead to an intimate, formal vegetable garden enclosed by 6 feet-high glass walls. A concrete "pier" crosses the sand to the porch and front door which face the cliffs and look on to the courtyard garden, perhaps the only "suburban" element in the whole design. The hall follows the curved glass wall and opens dramatically into the spacious living room, with its exposed roof beams and expansive view of the ocean. Along the beach side of the house is a small sitting room shaded by lattice work and a low-ceilinged dining room, both providing more private areas from the living room which through its mahogany and glass doors is almost part of the beach.

In his bid to design authentically Californian architecture, the choice of materials has always been a key issue for Quigley. The stucco and concrete vernacular of early twentieth-century Californian architects, like his mentor Irving Gill, has become his trademark. Here, the two-story structure consists of a poured-in-place concrete spine with cantilevered concrete floor slabs. A traditional wood frame clad in black asphalt shingles is used for the bedroom wing. Two guest bedroom suites above the garage are fronted by an asphalt shingle screen. The exposed concrete provides attractive sculptural and geometric shapes both inside and outside: a majestic setting for the fireplace, different levels and walkways in the sand, the striking deco-like concrete spine and so on. As a counter balance to the expanses of concrete and glass, a series of redwood lattice structures, stained grey, are used for cladding or for shade and privacy. Reminiscent of original beach huts, they are just one of the many elements that make this elegant Beach House a truly Californian building.

132

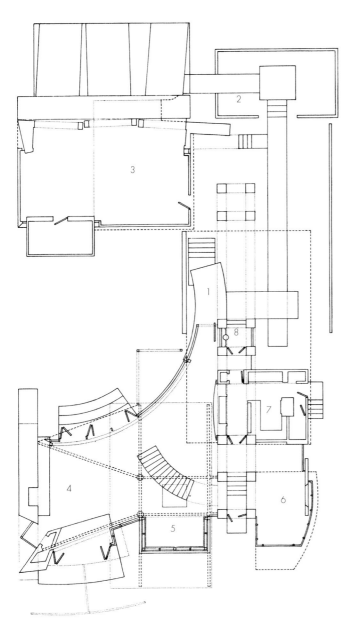

Lower floor.

1. Entrance.
2. Vegetable garden.
3. Garage.

4. Living room.
5. Sofa area.
6. Diming room.
7. Kitchen.
8. Bathroom.

San Diego architect Rob Quigley has always believed in a celebration of local architecture, and firmly rejected the Eurocentric bias of American architecture. Conscious of the geographical context of California he looks south, across the Mexican border, and out west across the Pacific for his inspiration. His construction materials are nearly always from the vernacular techniques – light wood frame and tilt-up concrete slab. His philosophy not only makes local architecture "fit" in its Californian context, but is also pragmatic in view of ever-decreasing budgets.

"The excitement of inhabiting the ocean's edge is translated into a series of architectural juxtapositions: thick walls of poured concrete against glass pavilions; deep shade and dappled light against the sand's harsh glare; exposed, stagelike decks and platforms against veiled privacy."
Rob Quigley

The house opens its spaces up to the seascape and extends its platforms ant over the sand.

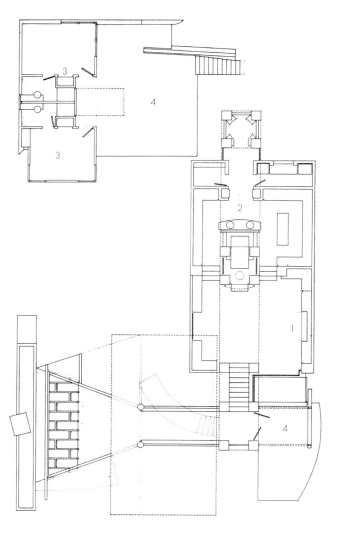

Upper floor.

1. Master bedroom.
2. Main bathroom.
3. Quest rooms.
4. Terrace.

"In a country that is fast minimizing the
differences among cultures and regions,
the search for a locally meaningful
architecture is more and more relevant...
As the larger built environment shrinks and
homogenizes, the need for architects to
define the particular and capture the spirit
of the place becomes critical."
Rob Quigley

Greeneny and light combine
to create the architecture.

The sweeping staircase of wood and steel
leads to the mid-level sundeck. A private
bridge at the top of the stairs leads to the
back of the house along the concrete spine.

Capistrano Beach House

Location: Capistrano Beach, California, USA.

Completion date: 1994.

Architect: Rob Wellington Quigley.

Collaborators: Teddy Cruz, Catherine Herbst
(design team), Integrated Structural Design
(structural consultants), Mark Falcane
(general contrator).

Photographer: Undine Pröhl.

Peter Gluck

Just a many farmhouse have become purely domestic homes rather than working farms, so has the relationship of their occupants with the natural surroundings evolved. They see it as an object of leisure and contemplation rather than a source of income or survival. Farmers have always had a pragmatic attitude, and as in this early nineteenth-century farmhouse in Millerton, New York, it was typical to build the house right on the road for better access to the market towns. Similarly, there was none of the contemporary interest in linking the interior of the home with the exterior – indoor life would be more inward-looking and focused on the kitchen range. In this case there was no seeking out the nearby pond, waterfall and apple orchard, which were both invisible and inaccessible.

With a brief to extend this farmhouse for a family of four with growing children, New York architect Peter Gluck's approach was to re-establish the house's relationship with its environment. His late twentieth-century solutions counterbalanced the early nineteenth-century shortcomings. The eighty-foot extension stretches away from the existing house, turning its back on the road and getting deeper into the countryside. It also connects the home directly with the landscape by following the natural slope and arriving at the pond area: the way the building resolves the change in level in its course to eventually become single storey is gracefully handled. Also an exterior walkway on the upper level makes it possible to walk from the original house to the pond.

The new wing is a pure linear shape, in bold contrast to the old farmhouse with its tacked-on parts. Its ninety-foot metal shed roof encloses the whole program, unifying the composition and allowing changes in the form below it not to interfere with the overall control of the composition. Though the difference is striking, the simple geometry and strong lines seem to complement the old house, and the extension is reminiscent of traditional farm outbuildings. The new roof overlaps at either end covering a terrace on the upper level of the old house and forming a covered porch at its end. This reinforces the esthetics of haylofts and barns.

The difficult problem of linking old and new is resolved with the construction of a single-story link, which is used as a transition area. The new extension can then be an uncompromised single volume, like the original house. A new kitchen has been built in this space so that the two buildings are united in day-to-day living terms. However the two roofs are separate: the gap between the gable end of each marks the division of old and new, and at the same time sets up a relationship between them; furthermore one of the tall timber posts supporting the new gable comes down outside the single-story volume, creating subtle interlocking effect.

The structural rationale behind the design is a series of eightbays giving a flexibility of room sizes, openings and enclousures. The rooms occupy the entire 14-foot width of the extension. Within this simple geometry different rooms have been created – a studio, master bedroom and children's room. This building has more industrial, larger, tougher feel about it with its steel staircase, metal roof and chimneys and larger panes of glass: a reflection of technological advances since the nineteenth century as well as the changing demands of the inhabitants.

Linear House is a classic example of the "contextual modernism" practised by Peter Gluck. As in similar projects of his, he has managed to create something contemporary which is at the same time sensitive to the original and to its setting, a building that complements it without imitating or overshadowing it.

Linear House is an exemplary house in Peter Gluck's series of projects in "contextual" modernism, which along with his "masked" modernism and "bold" modernism have been the thread running through his recent work. In his words: "this design confronted two contexts: one of landscape, the other of ordinary vernacular style. The simple, metal shed roof of the addition echoes the utilitarian aspect of the rural idiom, and the new exterior walkway…uses the topography the way local barns once gave easy access to the hayloft."

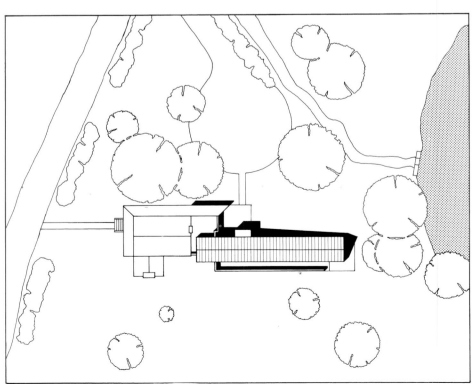

The 80-foot extension is a simple, elegant solution for enlarging this nineteenth-century farmhouse to accommodate a growing family. The two glass facades are hung on a rationalist post and beam structure. The waterfall on one side and the newly-created rock garden on the other can be seen from every room, as the building is one room deep.

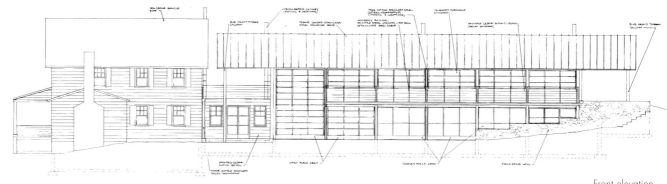

Front elevation.

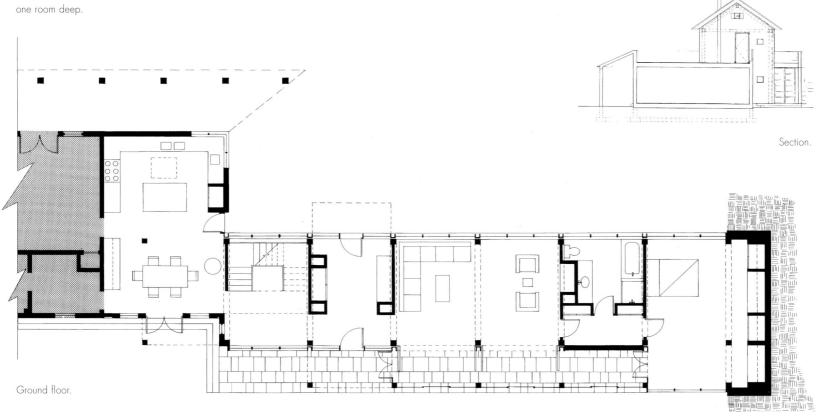

Section.

Ground floor.

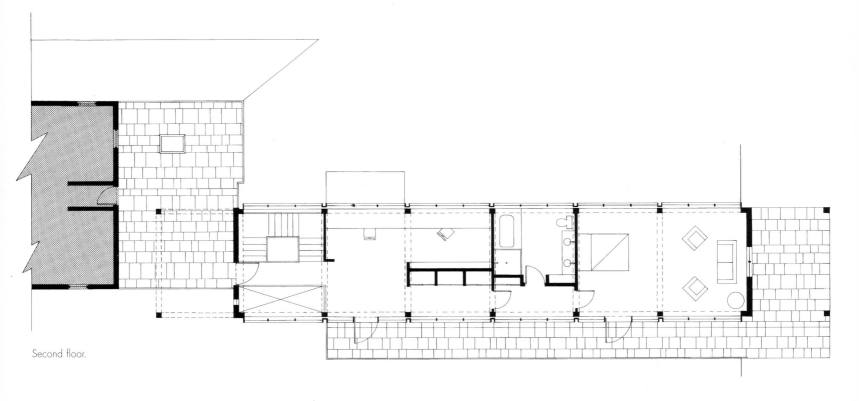

Second floor.

Construction detail (in plan) of partition wall embedded in facade.

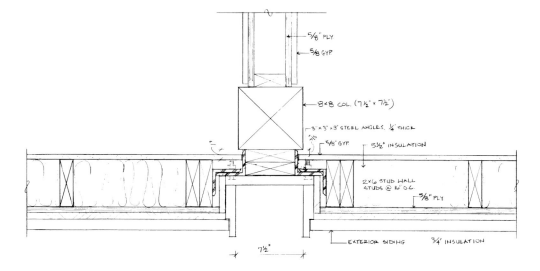

5/8" PLY
5/8" GYP
8×8 COL. (7½" × 7½")
3" × 3" × 3" STEEL ANGLES, ½" THICK
5/8" GYP
5½" INSULATION
2×6 STUD WALL STUDS @ 16" O.C.
5/8" PLY
EXTERIOR SIDING   ¾" INSULATION
7½"

The interior detailing is bold and contemporary. The stairwell is very generous. A bridge from the top of the steel stairs links the terrace above the link building to the upper floor of the new building.

There are various references to the vernacular tradition in the use of materials: large timbers, cedar siding and the form reminiscent of farm buildings. In addition there is a certain Japanese serenity, an influence from Gluck's years working in Japan which often comes out in his designs.

Linear House

Location: Millerton, New York, U.S.A.

Date of construction: 1996.

Architect: Peter Gluck.

Collaborators: Suki Dixon (project manager).

Photographer: Paul Warchol.

Gabriel Poole

Australian architect Gabriel Poole is currently enjoying the flattering attentions of the international architectural media, who have suddenly realised he has been responsible for some remarkable buildings and has a proven track record of innovative design solutions. His Poole House shows that, though in his sixites now, his past energy is not faltering. On the contrary he is still breaking new ground. At the same time he is elder statesman enough to stand back "to give the younger ones a go", and refuses to submit it to the State Chapter awards, despite predictions of success; after all he already has various prestigious awards to his name, including a Boyd Award in 1990 for his Eummundi Tent House. Some of his former pupils, such as John Mainwaring, are now leading lights in Australian architecture, yet Poole still has a lot to teach the younger generations.

Situated at Lake Weyba on the Sunshine Coast, Queensland, this house embodies many of the features characteristic of Poole's work. It shows him to be an innovative thinker, a pragmatist and an environmentalist - perhaps the perfect profile for clients selecting an architect. He should know, as he is both client and architect on this job. It is a personal product, but at the same time a building that could be a prototype for public housing, being affordable and environmentally sound. Affordable is generally synonymous with ordinary, but as Poole says this house is an example of how "ordinary people can suddenly afford an extraordinary house".

The Pooles regarded this beautiful unspoilt site as their haven; they camped on it for two years, slowly evolving the design according to the light, sun, winds, natural surroundings and so on.

The site was of paramount importance to them and they were anxious to preserve it as they found it. The house "touches lightly on the ground" in true aboriginal spirit, showing it due respect. At the same time the rooms are designed to get maximum benefit from the natural surroundings. Made up of three pavilions with sharply pitched roofs, it has a nomadic quality like an encampment; the landscape is established but the housing is more transient. It is this ephemeral lightness in Poole's work that has captured the imagination of Europeans and North Americans.

The pavilions are a new direction for Poole. Connected by wooden footbridges they have distinct roles: the first, also the entrance, is the widest and most public, containing the living area - kitchen/dining room, lounge and office. Although partly divided there is a sense of one large space, especially when the front windows are fully opened so they merge with the large, covered deck. The second pavilion, totally devoted to the bath area, is pure indulgence: a sunken pool demands idle contemplation of the landscape that stretches out beyond the nearly open wall, looking east. On the same wall the shower, lined in galvanised steel, juts on to another wooden deck shaded by a delicate, Japanese-style canopy - an ideal spot for drying in the morning sun. The third pavilion houses the master bedroom.

Attractive and innovative but also practical and economical. A great deal of attention has been paid to heat and ventilation, making the house thermally efficient. Roof and ceilings are a twin wall mould resistant PVC with a 50cm gap between them to allow for heat dissipation. The rooms are very luminous but do not become overheated. Poole describes it as a solar house, opening everything up during the day, and closing it down at night with ventilation through insect screens; in the winter the steel roller garage doors on the north wall of each pavilion act as radiators when closed. Galvanised sheet, used extensively inside and outside, is also very appropriate for this environment. This is architecture of place, with a future in other places. The steel "C"- section frame is slender and lightweight but sturdy, being welded together and looping right around; it is sheathed in polycarbonate, steel and ply.

Poole Residence

When Gabriel and Elizabeth Poole found this unspoilt site, 10 kms east of Noosa Heads in Queensland, with its wallum grass, casuarinas and eucalyptus, he declared "The rolling stone stops here". For them it is the perfect haven and they have treated it with due respect. The slender, steel-framed structures sit delicately above the ground and do not intrude on the landscape.

The house is organised with three pavilions which are open the south.

It is affordable housing such as this that holds the key to architecture's future. This sort of construction is accessible to the broad populace because it is far less likely to drive them to financial ruin.

Poole House is a prototype of inexpensive, flexible housing: it can be built anywhere and be adapted to different social or cultural requirements.

Gabriel Poole's mission is "to take architecture to the people", something he feels architecture has failed to do. The future of the profession could depend on this kind of pragmatic and innovative thinking.

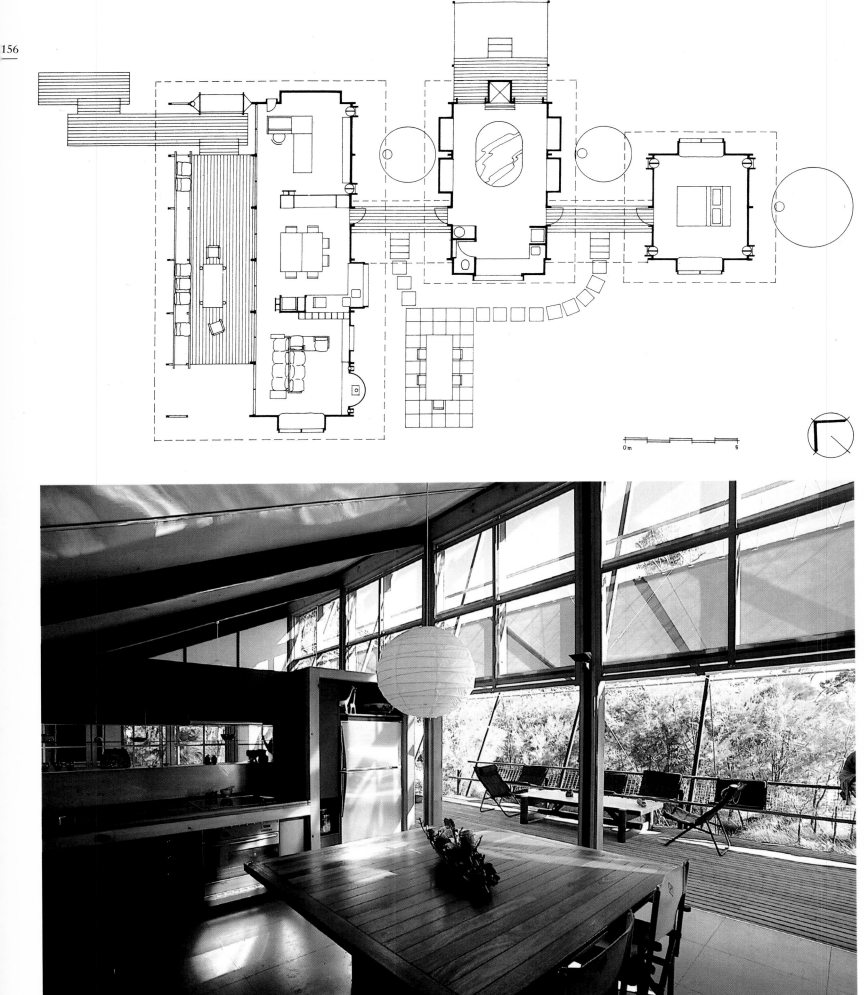

0 m   5

As Poole says "It's a design concept which I hope would appeal because it is so inexpensive to construct and gives tremendous flexibility and choices in line with cultural issues.
Less expensive versions should become available because the blueprint is here. Ordinary people can suddenly afford an extraordinary house.

Gabriel Poole's work shows many aspects which are characteristic of a traditional Japanese use of space. A horizontal tendency, the possibility of being opened to the landscape, spatial continuity and the use of natural light are devices which are used and reinterpreted by Poole until achieving the desired effects.

Wherever possible the interior opens out to
the exterior. In the front pavilion the
counterbalanced steel and vinyl panels fully
open so the rooms give onto the covered
deck, almost doubling the internal space.

In the bathroom, only a shower set in the wall prevents it from
fully opening to the landscape beyond; it feels as if it is an
exterior space. It is as if the Pooles, after two years of camping
on the site, still want to open up their tent flaps and commune
with their beautiful surroundings.

Poole Residence

Location: Noosa Heads, Australia.

Completion date : 1996.

Architect: Gabriel Poole.

Collaborators: Elisabeth Poole (design),

Rod Bligh-Bligh Tanner (structure),

Barry Hamlet (aluminium).

Photographer: Peter Hyatt.

Stremmel Residence

Mark Mack

Some recent examples of architecture demonstrate a tendency to emphasize restraint over exuberance, reduction over redundancy, unity over dispersion, and local simplicity over transculturalism. The United States, whose architecture has been largely characterized by ostentatious projects financed by large companies, has recently seen the rise of several architects who have returned to a simpler style of architecture.

Mark Mack, who was born in Austria but lives in the United States, is one of these architects. His projects give priority to simplicity and clarity of purpose, and his bold use of shapes, colors and textures produces surprising and original effects. The economy of his style is often reminiscent of the mysticism of other American architects such as Wright or Kahn.

The Stremmel residence is located in the outskirts of Reno, practically in the desert. A simple glance at the results is enough to prove that quality in architecture does not depend on opulence or grandeur. The project demonstrates that Mack's primary considerations are the climate, vegetation, colors and building materials, rather than showy displays of technology or style. Mack's confidence in his mastery of these aspects, which form the real basis of architecture, allow him to eschew any flamboyant exhibitions of technique.

Mack's work contrasts with the faceless, anonymous buildings of glass and steel that are so common in modern architecture. Life in these showcase buildings can be a form of torment for their inhabitants, who feel like prisoners in a cold inhospitable environment. Mack's answer to these glass cages is a style of architecture on a human scale which emphasizes warmth, protection, and comfort. Walls regain their strength, independence and dignity. His "spaces", which are as much interior as exterior, are constructed with emotions and feelings in mind.

Light, which is usually lateral, reflected, or filtered, produces colorful effects designed to influence the inhabitants' state of mind. Water constitutes a fundamental element of the project. Like an oasis, it stands in opposition to the arid surroundings and influences the color and shape of the project, which act like unpredictable boundary markers for the space.

In a way, the Stremmel residence reproduces the arrangement found in traditional houses built around a central patio containing a swimming pool or pond. The house is built on a concrete platform that serves to mark the limits of the residence. This is Mack's response to the challenge of constructing a micro-environment which stands apart from the enormous, barren void of the desert. Mack works within this parallelepiped, creating and delimiting volumes which he carefully interconnects. The result is a floating, fluid space, both interior and exterior at the same time. It is this effect that gives the entire project its character and internal logic.

Single-family houses are exceptional specimens for analyzing the domestic dreams and ambitions of our times. They reflect the fantasies of their inhabitants as well as the creative abilities of the architects. The customer requires the architect to give shape to his vague aspirations, whereas the architect needs the customer's fantasies to spark his imagination and create a new chapter in his professional biography.

Stremmel Residence

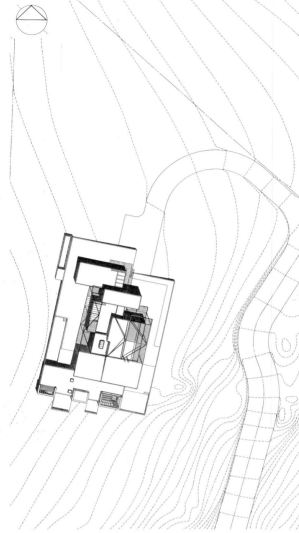

Site plan.

The Stremmel residence sits on top
of a concrete platform that rises
up from ground level.

The water and the lawn mark the
end of the parched desert and
the beginning of the residence.

The different colors, shapes and
textures serve to configure the
various volumes and distinguish
them from one another.

East elevation.

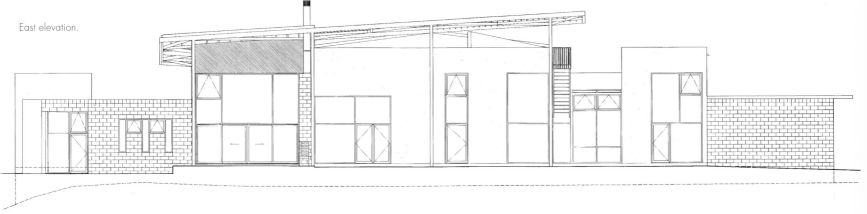

Mack's protective and
eminently livable architecture is
designed on a human scale.

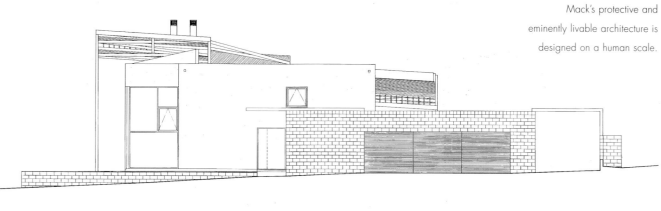

South elevation.

North elevation.

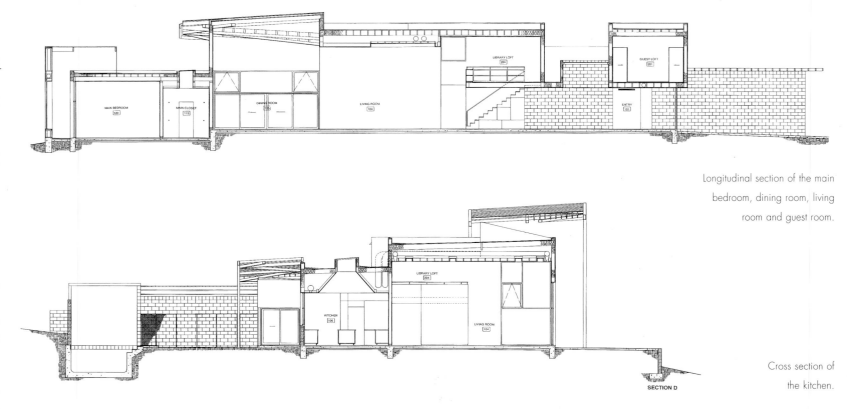

Longitudinal section of the main bedroom, dining room, living room and guest room.

Cross section of the kitchen.

The interior volumes are interconnected in such a way that they create a floating, fluid space which is simultaneously interior and exterior.

The interiors are notable for their simplicity, integrity, and clarity of purpose.

General floor.

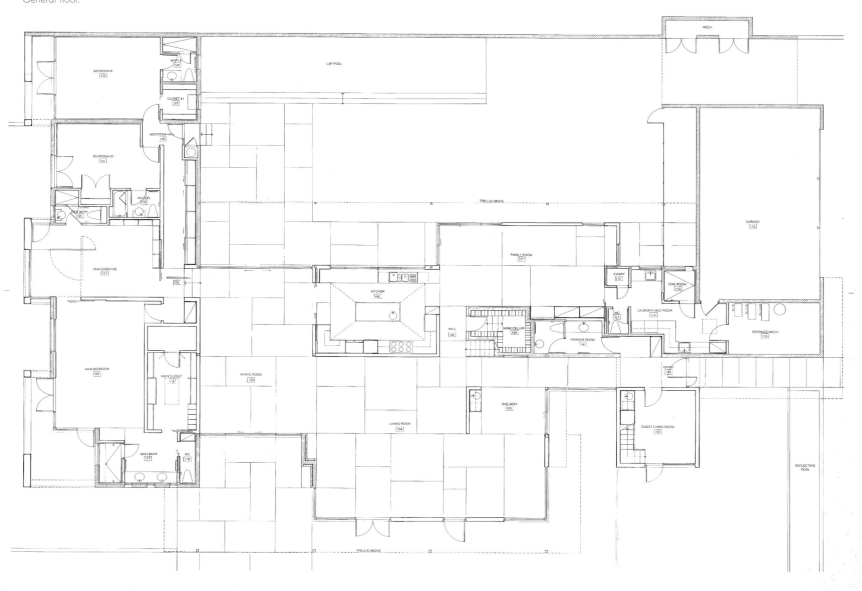

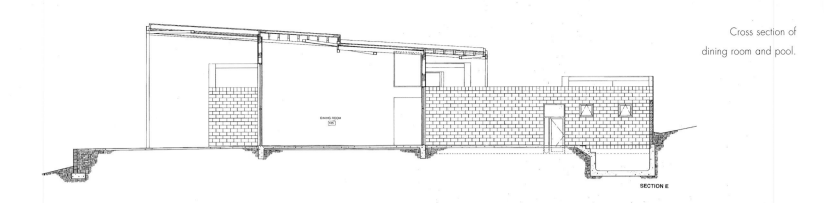

SECTION E

Stremmel Residence

Location: Reno, Nevada, U.S.A.

Construction date: 1995.

Architect: Mark Mack.

Photographer: Undine Pröhl.

Residence Stremmel
e Stremmel
remmel Residence Stremmel
Stremmel Residence Stremmel
idence Stremmel
mel Residence Stremmel
mmel Residence Stremmel
esidence Stremmel
Stremmel Residence Stremmel
dence Stremmel
mel Residence Stremmel
mel Residence Stremmel Stremmel

House in Celaya

Grupo LBC

This elegant pavilion sits on top of a small hill on the plain of the San Rafael ranch, in the suburbs of Celaya. The ranch provides facilities for horseback riding, including indoor and outdoor hippodromes and stables for thirty horses.

The pavilion looks down on the main course, which lies near a dense wood of trees, some of which are over a hundred years old. At first glance, it appears to be a metaphor for the white hurdles that line the fields and stand out against the many shades of green in the well-kept landscape. The "white hurdles" of the pavilion are the metal beams mounted on thick cylindrical columns. These are separated from the two buildings and serve a double function. Esthetically, they provide a visual link between the buildings and the landscape. On a more functional level, they support the tense, light canvas awnings that give shade to the terraces and facades, which serve as outdoor sitting rooms, ideal for watching the activity on the courses.

The project consists of two pavilions apparently joined, but at the same time separated, by a reflecting pool. The pool fulfills a practical as well as an esthetic function, since it increases the humidity and gives a feeling of freshness in a dry climate that can easily reach temperatures of 104° Fahrenheit. The smaller pavilion holds a bedroom measuring 538 square feet with a bathroom and dressing room of 270 square feet. The larger pavilion consists of a 754 square-foot living room as well as a kitchen and bathroom. Both the living room and bedroom are extraordinarily spacious and are visually connected to the side terraces through the windows. Because they are so open to the outside, the real size of these rooms is not limited to the indoors, but encompasses the landscape outside.

The pavilions are connected by footbridges made of unvarnished wood which cross the pool at water level. They are covered by vaulted roofs that allow them to reach a considerable height at the center without destroying the cozy effect of the project.

The two pavilions are completely independent of one another. They face each other at the front, where the service rooms and chimneys are located. Although both buildings have large windows, they are placed on the facade that looks out onto the courses in an east-west axis. From one side of the garden it is possible to see the landscape on the other side, but it is practically impossible to see the other pavilion. The owners seem to have wanted to have two separate houses, one for themselves and one for guests. In the end, the pool and the footbridges separate the two pavilions, rather than uniting them.

House in Celaya

Longitudinal section.

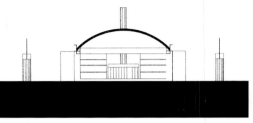

Cross section.

This residence received first prize in the Biennial Mexican Architecture competition in 1996 in the one-family house category.

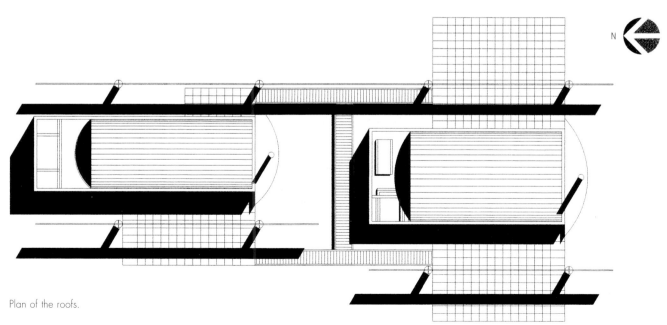

N

Plan of the roofs.

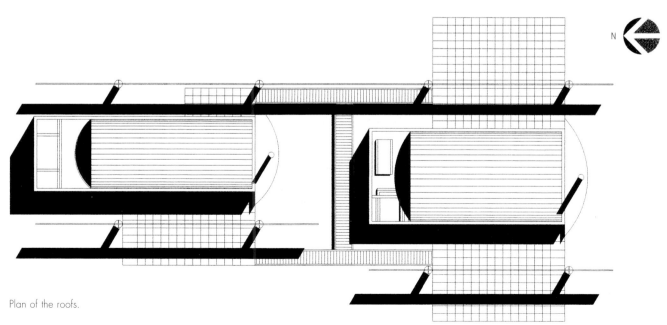

Although there is no fence to
separate the residence from the
hippodrome, the metal beams
delimit the residential space.

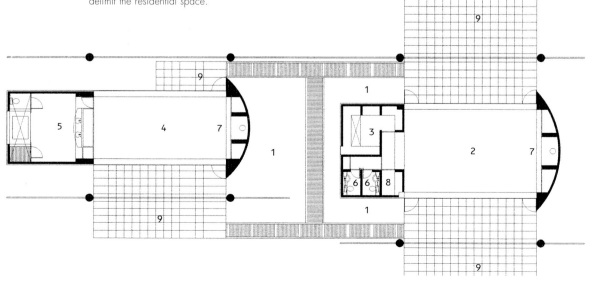

Ground plan.

1. Reflecting pool.
2. Living room-dining room.
3. Kitchen.
4. Master bedroom.
5. Main bathroom.
6. Half-bathroom.
7. Fireplace.
8. Wine cellar.
9. Terrace.

The vaulted roof is completely smooth, without skylights or ventilation grates. All of the closets are built into the walls, so that the room is left uncluttered, with only the tables and chairs. The side windows are fixed directly to the walls without any carpentry work. Access is provided by one sole door in the corner.

The travertine pavement provides a sense of continuity between the interior and the terraces on both sides.

House in Celaya

Location: Celaya, Guanajuato, Mexico.

Completion date: 1994.

Architects: Alfonso López Baz, Javier Calleja Ariño.

Collaborators: Guillermo Flores, Octavio Cardoza,

Arturo Hernandez (structure).

Photographer: Fernando Cordero.

Kappe Tamuri Residence

Kappe Studio

This 3800 square foot house and studio was built on a downsloping 1.5 acre semi-rural site in the ruggedly beautiful Topanga Canyon area of Los Angeles County. The project was built as the Architects' family home and work place.

The main wing of the house is a large, two-story, shoebox-type space, a basic rectangular shape with operations from back to front to affect its spatial characteristics. This section of the house is oriented parallel to the slope of the land and seems to emerge from the hillside. Inside, the painted colors and materials are rich and warm reflecting tones of the surrounding canyon. The main social rooms are here in one continuous space overlaid in part by the main bedroom, study and catwalk. The kitchen is central and open, minimally defined by the island cabinet, lights and catwalk above. The dining table is situated opposite the kitchen. Again, subtle but clear use of the architecture reinforces the otherwise transparent room. Unquestionably, this is the most stunning room in the house. Somehow, Kappe and Tamuri have achieved a space which during the day, with its glass walls and ceiling so high, seems to be outside, like a ledge on an exposed cliff. While at night the glass darkens and the redwood catwalk is lit from below shrinking and centering the room, making it an intimate camp in front of its fire.

The Bedroom/Studio wing is oriented parallel to the topography of the site and is anchored by a 10' wide lateral core situated between two block walls. The core consists of baths, laundry and mechanical room. The three zones of the solar assisted hydronic floor heating system eminate from this core. Laid against this 10' strip is the Studio at grade level and the Bedrooms above. All living spaces and even one of the baths open fluidly to decks and views which extend the interior spaces in ways that are hard to quantify.

The resulting angle between the two wings of the house is 102.5 degrees. Like a piece of a walled city, this open L layout allows for and shelters a large courtyard in front of the house. As shown on the site plan, the formal layout of the house reflects a desire for the inclusion of the architecture within the larger landscape. And although Kappe likens the plan form to a truck and trailer about to jackknife, he also admits that the fanning characteristic of the straight lines of the plan may behave in a parabolic manner - implying curvature and softness which seems to hold resonance with the formation of the canyon itself.

Details were generated which expressed the inherent characteristics of each primary building material without straying far from it's everyday useage. With careful combining, assemblage and construction, (done by Kappe), it was hoped that the perception of these basic building materials might be transformed. For example, the concrete block walls were all identically scored horizontally to emphasize their gravity-based nature. The patterned spacing even suggesting stone masonry or geotechnical strata. As well, the walls were sandblasted and terminated at the same elevation to maintain similarity and modulation. However, their separation and differing orientation gives a sense of shifted release and even randomness.

As the house pivots to become parallel to the slope, it is lifted off the ground, hung between the rigid steel frames and the block walls. This helped to achieve a compact building footprint and minimized grading. Cool air storage for natural ventilation was also established under the shadow of the building. To the south and east are views of the largely unspoiled canyon lands. Here the solid and void characteristics of the block walls and glass walls were studied carefully

Kappe Tamuri Residence

"A main goal of the design was to devise a unique pavilion or shell which could accommodate site conditions and the changing orientation of the house to its site. We began searching for a simple combination of structural parts that would allow great internal spatial freedom and envelope flexibility. Our solution needed to retain "road loads" from above, open out to views of unspoiled canyon lands to the south and east, pin through geotechnical slippage planes to the west and protect against fire and flood (not uncommon in the canyons of the Santa Monica Mountains)." Finn Kappe.

Behind the house, the more defensive or closed sides of the building respond to the boulevard to the north and a neighboring house to the west.

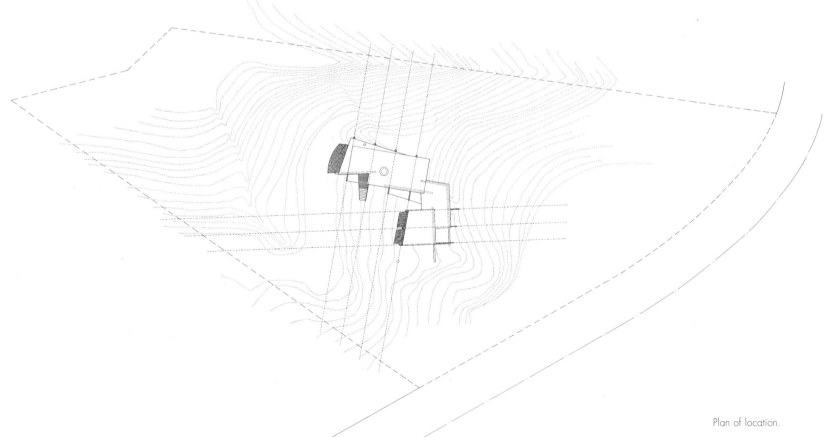

Plan of location.

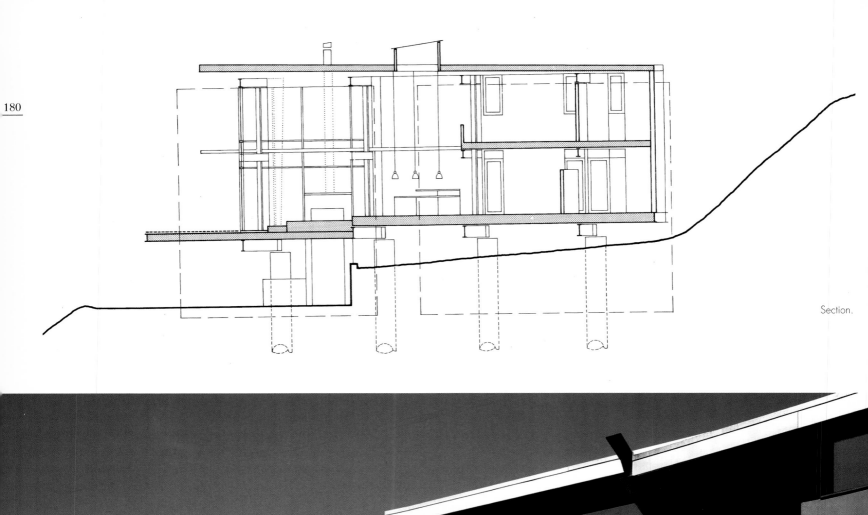

Section.

The large window in the entrance hall and the double height of the dining room make this an almost outside area. At night the interior light is reflected in the red wood panelling of the living room, creating a warm atmosphere.

Ground floor and
second floor.

1. Entrance.
2. Living room.
3. Kitchen.
4. Dinner room.
5. Sala familiar.
6. Store.
7. Studio.
8. Bedroom.

Both the owners and architects
were determined to achieve a
flow in the internal spaces. A
series of architectural features –
walls, beams, pillars,
balustrades – link up like the
notes of a melody.

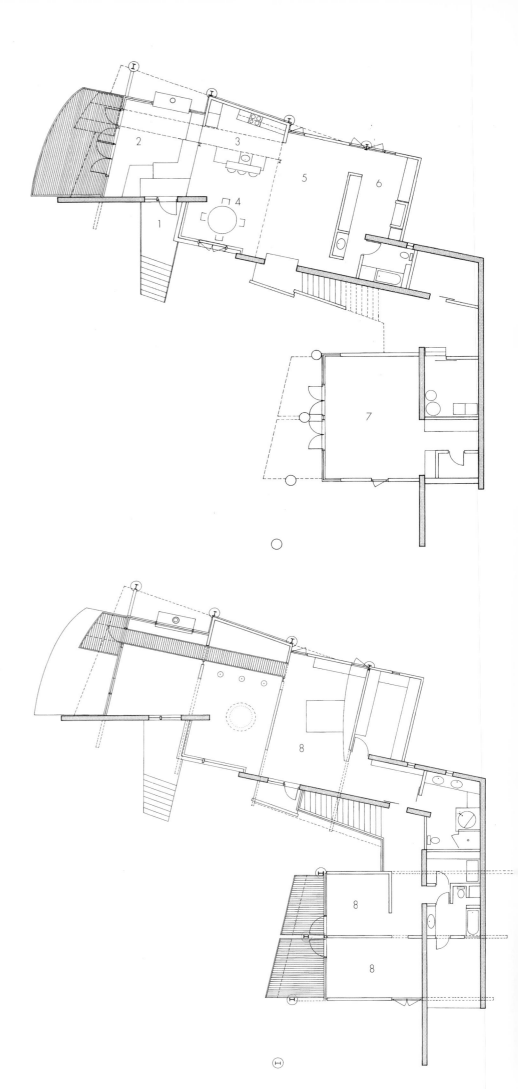

Kappe Tamuri Residence

Location: Topanga, California.

Completion date: 1997.

Architects: Finn Kappe, Maureen Tamuri.

Collaborators: Reiss, Brown, Ekmekji;

Woods Engineering (structural),

Richard Reiss (civil), Finn Kappe (lighting),

Finn Kappe (general contractor).

Photographers: David Hewitt/Anne Garrison

Architectural Photography.

House in Collserola

Joan Rodon

Fortunately, after the absurdities committed through the years, irreversibly harming the countryside in many cases, a new concept of architecture is emerging, one which is much more respectful to the natural setting and which tries to harmoniously integrate the buildings into the geography.

Such is the case of this single family dwelling by Joan Rodón located in the Collserola hills, one of the few remaining natural settings in the city of Barcelona. The house exhibits an advanced design, demonstrates a boldness of colour and achieves perfect integration in its setting.

The originality of the house is centred on its three storeys, which are superimposed following the line of the hillside where it is located. The rooms of the first two storeys of the building, whose total area is 254 sq.m., are connected by a double-height space between the living room and the study. On the lower level, a continuous space is formed, harbouring an ample vestibule, kitchen, dining room, a double-height living room, a T.V. room and a toilet. A study and a bedroom with a bathroom are situated on the second storey while the master bedroom, furnished with a dressing room and spacious bathroom, is located on the third.

This bedrom is arranged like a pergola located over the accessible roof and whose main volume is a cube from which spread plans which form the main openings. The different levels of the terrain have allowed the creation of ample terraces, where a barbeque has been constructed, and which serve as veritable exterior salons, keeping the porch and the garage at street level.

The architect wanted to play with and take maximum advantage of the light. He partially covered the double-height space with a jalousy which, in the morning, produces surpising light effects, reflects the setting sun in the afternoon and at night, inverts the effect to reflect the interior light like an enormous magical lantern.

The colour, administered with a certain dose of daring, also fulfills a double function: on one hand, it serves to give structure to the levels of the staggered walls which run from the house and along the terraces until the level of the garage and the street; and on the other hand, aesthetically shapes the building, adding strong doses of plasticity. The colour scheme has been conceived with mastery and risk, as if the understanding of an architect had come from the palette of a great painter: so colours as disparate as cobalt blue or fire engine red coexist in rare harmony with an intense yellow. On occasion, the colour also serves to shape the forms. Thus, one of the exterior stairways, of unfaced concrete, is splendidly carried off by the intense blue of the wall to which it is united, gaining in liveliness and acquiring a more ethereal appearance still. The same happens with the alternation between hot and cold colours: if the dwelling is observed from different angles, we find a preponderance of yellows and reds, which brilliantly bring the forms into relief, or of blues and whites that remind us of the geographic proximity of the Mediterranean. The vivid green of the lawn is the element which brings together the vibrant tones of the colour scheme and the more neutral ones such as that of the treated wood which paves the terraces.

If the colour brings a plastic quality to the house, the simplicity and beauty of the spaces give it a sculpted character with which new concepts are explored; the large cubes of the constructed spaces alternate with the empty spaces, mutually limiting and creating a harmonious dialogue between nature and art.

House in Collserola

Transversal section.

Colour throws the forms into relief.

The exterior stairs exhibit sculptural value.

Great care was taken with the Mediterranean vegetation covering the Collserola hills.

SECTION SITE

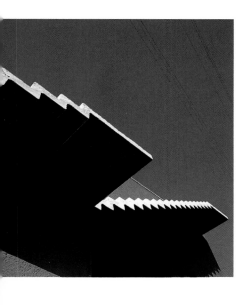

Concrete, wood and colour
are intergrated to perfection.
The dwelling is perfectly
adapted to the terrain.

Ground floor plan.

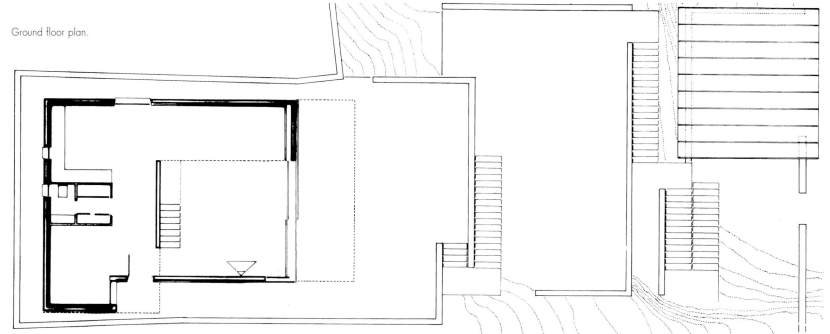

Plan of the 2 upper levels.

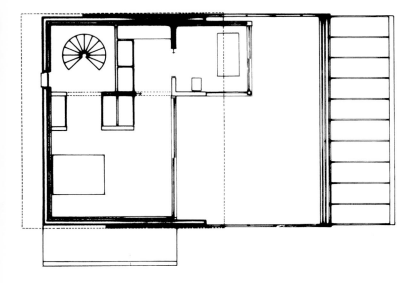
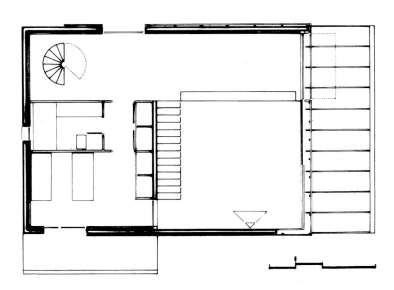

The project's privileged site.

The kitchen is situated in a continuous space on the lower level. The Mediterranean can be seen from the mountain.

The master bedroom lies within a cubic volume where the main openings are also located.

House in Collserola

Location: Barcelona, Spain.

Completion date: 1994.

Architect: Joan Rondon.

Collaborators: Sac Groc (building constructor).

Photographer: Eugèni Pons

Valor-Frutos-Sanmartín

Right from the beginning, this project was designed around the topography and location. On the one hand there was the extreme slope of the land; on the other, the almost triangular shape of the lot. Since local regulations stipulated that the house had to be placed at least 3 yards from the borders of the plot, there was very little choice about where to site it. The owners had also requested that the surrounding trees be left untouched, and that there be a swimming pool facing the scenery.

After building a series of containing walls in order to create a flat central patio, the house was constructed on a foundation of concrete pillars. These pillars form two contiguous squares, each measuring 20 x 20 feet. This gives each floor of the house an area of about 755 square feet.

The house faces south, which follows the slope of the land and affords an ideal view and excellent exposure to the sun. The building consists of one semi-basement floor and two double-height units, vertically superimposed. The lower unit holds the living area, while the higher contains the bedrooms.

Access to the estate is provided by a road which runs along the northern border of the lot. Since the road is higher than the patio, a bridge runs from the road to the middle floor of the house, which holds the garage and a vestibule. This floor acts as an intermediate step between the exterior and interior of the house, and divides it in half.

Visitors entering the house can choose between going down to the ground floor, which is visible from the railing of the double-height area over the living room, or going up to the bedrooms. In any case, the architects have clearly designed this space as a transition area. There are few openings in the walls, which means that the views gradually open up as we enter the main rooms of the house. This technique also allows the south wall of the house to regulate the temperature of the house naturally. A sheet of polycarbonate lets the sun's rays pass through and heat up an air chamber. The sun also heats a thermally insulated sheet of steel, which is painted black. The heat generated by the resulting greenhouse effect is transmitted to the water supply and piped into the living room and bedrooms via vents.

From outside, the architects wanted the house to have a unified, solid appearance that would not show the interior distribution of space or the functional aspects of the house. For this reason, none of the different-sized windows of the rooms are visible in the facade.

The south façade is composed of flat planes, either shutters, glass or polycarbonate. These sheets form horizontal bands which lean at different angles. The side facades are uniform surfaces covered in white stucco with almost no openings. Their appearance could be described as a simplified cross section of the house.

The north facade, which has no view, is covered with fretted metal sheeting. The same sheeting continues onto the curved roof, and even covers the windows, where it has been perforated to allow the passage of air and light. The resulting appearance is compact and abstract.

Coll-Vallés House

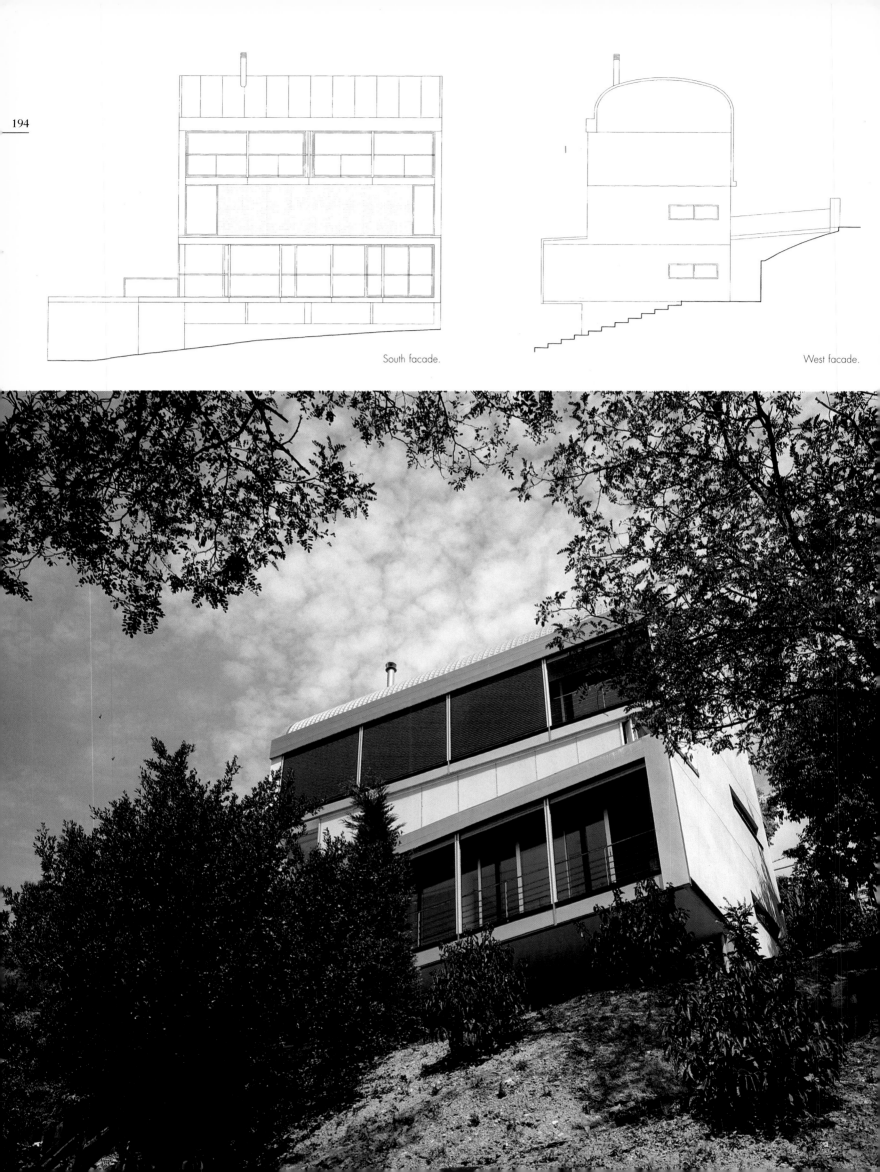

South facade.

West facade.

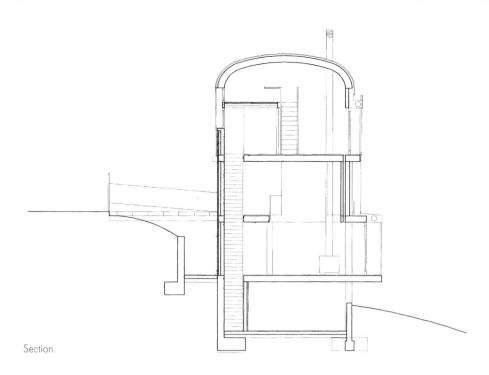

Section.

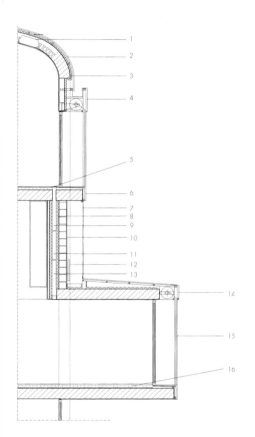

Construction section of the south facade.

1. Framework of the roof, made of self-guided beams and ceramic vaults.

2. Copperfield metal sheeting.

3. Insulation materials.

4. Aluminum sheeting.

5. Aluminum intake vent.

6. Aluminum sheeting.

7. Polycarbonate with 2 $^{1/2}$-inch air chamber.

8. 3-inch Celenit insulation.

9. Intake duct.

10. Galvanized sheet, painted black.

11. Exhaust duct.

12. Hot-water radiators, painted black.

13. Intake duct.

14. Facade and roof covered with aluminum sheeting.

15. Retractable shutters with adjustable blinds.

16. Under-floor heating.

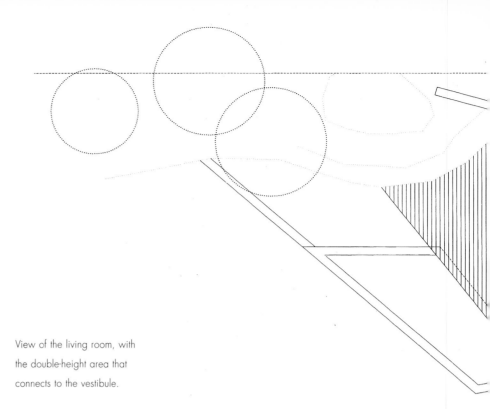

View of the living room, with the double-height area that connects to the vestibule.

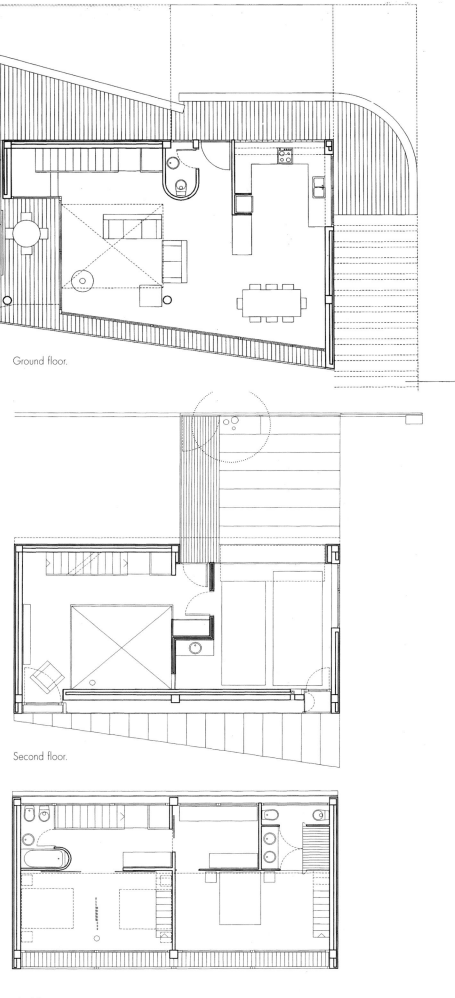

Ground floor.

Second floor.

Third floor.

Detail of the master bedroom,
showing the stairway which
leads up to a small
comfortable attic space above
the bathroom and below the
curved roof.

The kitchen is open to the dining
room and living room. For this
reason the architects continued their
use of finishes throughout.

The lighting can be varied by
means of the blinds on the shutters.
This produces various different
effects which change the way the
space is perceived.

Detail of the master bedroom. The
staircase leads to the small,
finished attic which lies between
the bathroom and the curved roof.

Coll-Vallés House

Location: Barcelona, Spain

Completion date: 1997.

Architects: Fidela Frutos, J.M. Sanmartín,
Jaume Valor.

Collaborators: Construcciones Técnicas Lliçà
(construction), Jarclos (landscaping), Alex Soler
(furniture).

Photographer: Eugeni Pons.

Collective Housing for the Cheesecake Consortium

Fernau & Hartman

It may not be everybody's idea of Shangri-La, but as an exercise in co-habitation and confronting the euphemistically-coined "Golden years", the "Cheesecake Consortium" is innovative, challenging and very admirable. As an architectural exercise it also represented a challenge for the Berkeley firm Fernau and Hartman, on many levels: from coping with eleven individuals as The Client to working within quite a modest budget. Happily a great deal of determination and goodwill on both sides helped the project to run smoothly and successfully, as several awards prove. One from the Californian branch of the A.I.A. described it as "a socially innovative, environmentally responsible and financially viable alternative for community living".

The idea behind the project was to build collective housing for a group of friends (4 couples and 3 singles), to be able to live together and give each other mutual support in the latter years of their lives. Currently in the forties to sixties age bracket, their friendships go back a long way and have been thoroughly tested. Most of them still work and live elsewhere but plan to retire here. Set in a 13-acre site in Mendocino County, north of San Francisco, the Cheesecake compound is built on a flat shelf in the 100-year- old flood plain of the Navarro River in the midst of a redwood forest. The apparently whimsical name actually belongs to the site: the previous owners were an Italian family named Casatas, loosely translated as "cheese pie" and adopted by the local community as "cheesecake".

Architects Richard Fernau and Laura Hartman are known for their imaginative, environmentally respectful projects and collaborative approach and for their keen interest in social issues. "We loved the idea of doing housing for a group. This was a project with modest financial parameters, and we welcomed the cost challenges." In turn they were impressed by the attitude of the group who were easier to deal with than a single client; decisions were democratic but kept tight and organized.

The compound has a youthful feel about it in appearance and spirit, like a camp or new settlement. Ironic considering its purpose, but a true reflection of the energy behind it. There are communal rooms for sundry activities and the partners plan to spend time hiking in the surrounding forests and playing volleyball. Nevertheless they are realistic about the future so the design includes such pragmatic details as 34-inch- wide doors for wheel chairs, space for ramps and an elevator. A thoughtful detail is the alternation of public and private spaces – for example to reach the laundry or library one passes the individual living quarters – which creates social circulation, avoiding any risk of one member becoming isolated.

There are three main buildings, raised five feet from the ground because of the flood plain, a bath house, a pool and tent platform and, in a separate clearing, a garden. The three main ones are the workshop, the lodge – housing communal kitchen, living room, dining room and office – and a bedroom wing that incorporates a library and laundry/sewing room. Interior space is over 5,000 square feet and exterior space in the form of verandas, a dog trot, tent decks and a pavilion total 3,000 square feet. Aware of the farm building ethic, but anxious not to fall into the picturesque, the architects designed a simple, inexpensive construction: a wood frame on concrete piers, with sidings of painted plywood and battens, stained cedar and painted corrugated metal. The roof is painted panel and unpainted corrugated metal. Where possible recycled materials were used: wood milled from the trees cleared on the site was used for the decking, banisters and dining table.

The communal spaces are all subtly designed to cope with large influxes of this enormous extended family (26 children and 9 grandchildren –to date...). Rooms spill out onto wide porches, guests can sleep on the tent platforms, or in the "dog-trot" wing (named after the southern tradition of roofed passages between structures). There is little likelihood of being neglected by your family here in this attractive and welcoming corner of Northern California. It is the antithesis of the conventional retirement home and the visitors will keep coming.

Site plan.

Fernau & Hartman divide the project up into different building. In this way, they manage to keep to a domestic scale in all the architectural elements and a more harmonious, less aggressive relationship with the landscape.

1. Workshop.

2. Lodge.

3. Pavilion.

4. Dog Trot.

5. Library.

6. Bath House.

7. Pool & Tent Platforms.

8. Garden.

Axonometry.

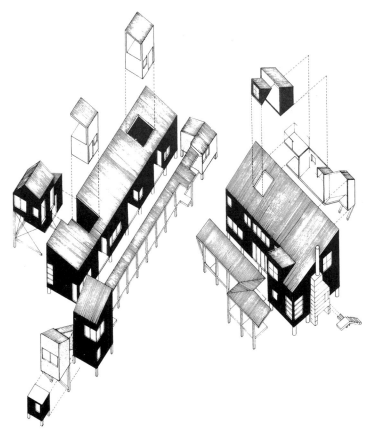

"....we were intrigued by the twist of retirement and cohousing. Philosophically, old age is one of the hardest issues to deal with. The Cheesecake group was grappling with life's largest problems – things people don't want to talk about – and at the same time they were making very practical decisions. It was a very powerful experience."
Richard Fernau

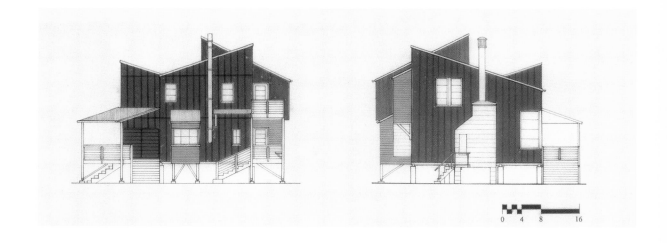

0   4   8   16

Main buildings' elevations.

The main lodge incorporates communal living room, dining room and 260 sq.ft. kitchen, and office as well as two apartments on the upper floor. The bedroom wing, known as the "dog-trot" because of its covered passageway, houses five apartments, a library upstairs and a laundry/sewing room. The third building is a workshop for projects, hobbies and tinkering.

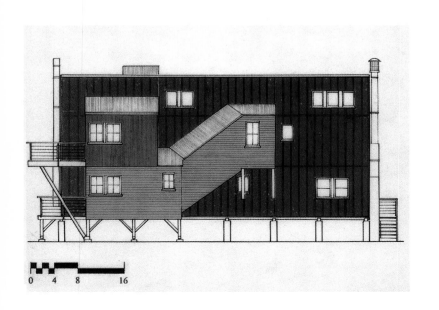

First floor.

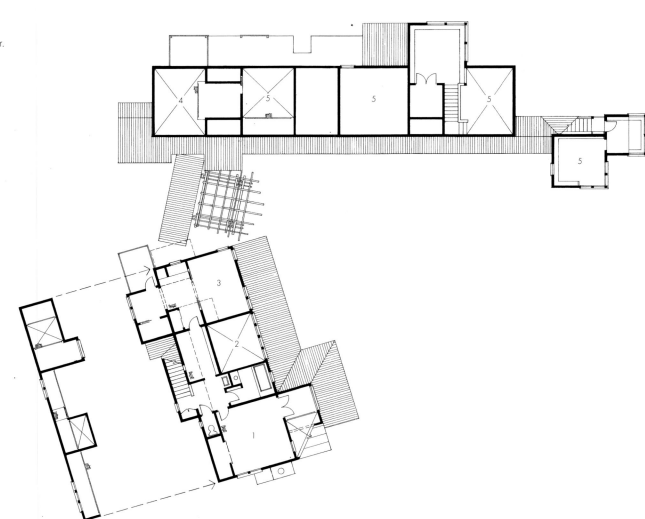

The different interior functions are colour-coded on the exterior cladding of the buildings' making an unusual, lively aesthetic. The basic structure is in plywood siding with vertical battens, and painted dark green, while common spaces are in yellow-stained bevel cedar siding. Supplementary private spaces are clad in red corrugated metal.

Ground floor.

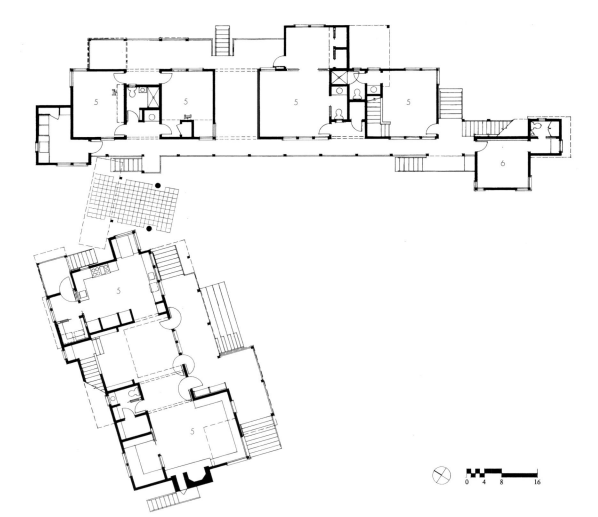

1. Living room.
2. Dining room.
3. Kitchen.
4. Laundry.
5. Bedroom.
6. Library.

0 4 8 16

Collective Housing for the

Cheesecake Consortium

Location: Mendocino Country, California.

Completion date: 1994.

Architects: Richard Fernau, Laura Hartman,

David Kau.

Collaborators: Tim Gray, Kimberly Moses,

Emily Stussi (team project),

Dennis McCroskey (structure), William Mah

Engineers (mechanical), Zieger Engineers

(electricity), Jim Boudoures (contractor).

Photographer: Richard Barnes.

e Housing for the Cheesecake Consortium. g el Cheesecake Consortium Collective Housing for the ke Consortium Collective Housing for the um Collective Housing for the Cheesecake Consortium r the Cheesecake Consortium ake Consortium Collective Housing for the Cheesecake Consortium Collective Housing for the Cheesecake Collective Housing for the Cheesecake Consortium Collective Housing ole Consortium Collective Housing for the Cheesecake for the Cheesecake Consortium Collective Housing for the heesecake Consortium Collective Housing for the Cheesecake Consortium Collective Housing for the Cheesecake Consortium

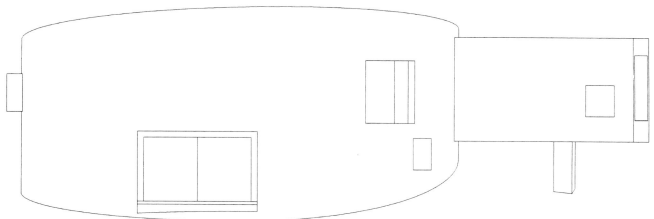

Villa in the Forest

Kazuyo Sejima

A house is the only refuge from the horror of emptiness, darkness and our obscure origins. It contains everything mankind has accumulated patiently over time and stands in opposition to escape, loss and absence as it imposes its own internal structure. Its very freedom lies in the fact that it is stable and closed, rather than vague and limitless. This villa in the Tateshina forest marks off an area of defense against the enormity of the woods and imposes a territory for human identity with the chaos of nature. Kazuyo Sejima chooses a circular layout to express the feeling of homogeneity that the forest evokes. The lush vegetation of the environment, which filters most of the sunlight through its branches, makes it difficult to determine a central axis and confuses our sense of direction.

The customer, a Tokyo art dealer, wanted a house to use as a second residence. The construction would need to incorporate a studio and exhibition area and should be suitable for receiving guests. The resulting project is arranged around a circular area in the center which serves as the studio/exhibition area, with the rest of the customary household functions distributed in a ring around it.

This arrangement creates an interior and exterior route which enhances the feeling of mobility in the house. The overall impression produced by the structure is that architecture is mainly a container which acts as a guide for movement. The inevitable result of this is a feeling of emptiness.

The house is organized around a luminous circular void which is visually and physically accessible through certain slots. This inner circle occupies the space that would traditionally contain the fireplace. Rather than providing heat, the space acts as a symbolic focal point and light source. The fireplace was once the warm, crackling soul of the house, the nucleus which gathered the inhabitants together and acted as a center for conversation and social life. Here, it is first individualized and then fragmented into a multitude of personal fires. Sejima has reproduced the arrangement of the first cabins where domestic life revolved around a central focal point, which in this case is art.

The perimeter of the circle is broken at various points to create an entrance, patio, or terrace. These are the areas where the line separating the interior from the exterior becomes blurred, and these spaces soften the transition and protect us from the forest, while at the same time hiding the domestic life inside. These openings are often considered mere holes in the wall, with no substance of their own. However, they perform many essential functions, such as climate control, security, or privacy. Because of this, they can be considered real "places" in their own right, each full of attributes and susceptible to being occupied in different ways.

For Sejima, this project can only develop through its form. Architecture consists of creating new forms that originate from the underlying concept and interact with the environment. Any project for a new house springs from the desire to create a new space, which in turn needs its own spirit or soul. A house is at once both a choice and a remorse, an exercise in power and servitude, a face and its mask, a protective shield and the perfect target.

A house is many things: an architect who strives to create something eternal, interior decoration applied to the labyrinths of psychology, new materials employed to brighten the spirit. All of these elements make a house a construction built on the space between desire and fulfillment.

Villa in the Forest

Sejima employs a circular layout to express the feeling of homogeneity produced by the vastness of the forest.

The project is laid out around the central circle that holds the studio and exhibition area and acts as a luminous focal point for the house.

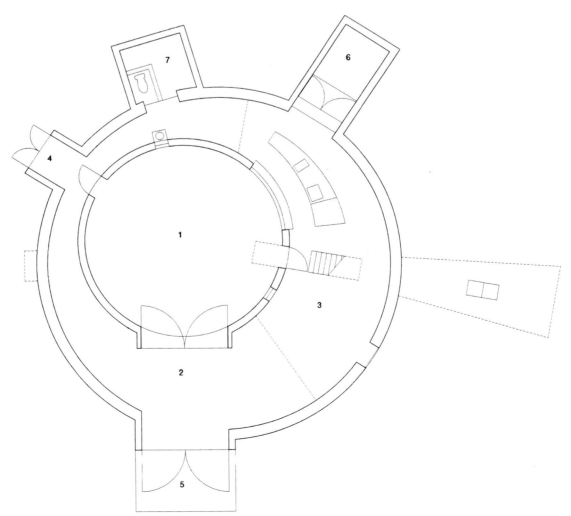

1. Workshop.
2. Living room.
3. Dining room.
4. Entrance.
5. Terrace.
6. Courtyard.
7. Storage.
8. Void.
9. Bedroom.
10. Bathroom.
11. Platform.

The dining room, kitchen and
living room are distributed
along the perimeter, creating
a continuous route of
circulation around the house.

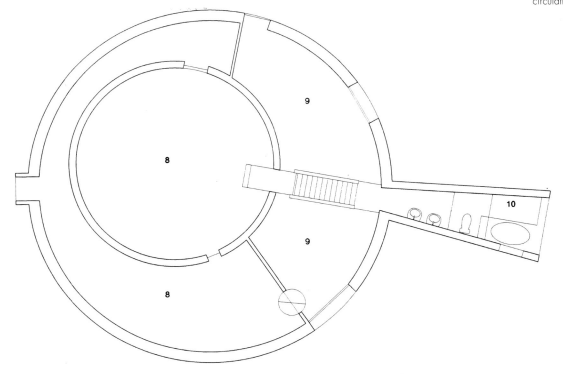

Villa in the forest

Location: Chino, Nagano Prefecture, Japan.

Date of construction: 1994.

Architect: Kazuyo Sejima.

Collaborators: Ryue Nishizawa, Sachiko Funaki (design), Matsui Gengo + O.R.S (structure).

Photographer: Nacasa & Partners.

the forest Villa in the forest
Villa in the forest
e forest Villa in the forest
est Villa in the forest
Villa in the forest
e forest Villa in the forest
lla in the forest
the forest
forest Villa in the forest
est Villa in the forest
the forest Villa in the forest

House in Tateshina

Iida Archischip Studio

The house is located in a resort area at the foot of Mount Tateshina in Nagano. The terrain slopes gently towards the southwest, and a forest surrounds the house.

As Iida himself explains, a vacation home is not subject to the same hierarchies as a first residence. The relationships between members are more relaxed. Different activities can often take place in the same place, since they do not require as much isolation and concentration. Finally there is generally a closer relationship with nature, since vacationers usually want to enjoy life in the outdoors. For this reason, many of the most innovative and compelling architectural works take the form in this type of homes, since the owners' needs and desires require more open spaces with a less conventional layout.

Iida's project takes shape from a basic design consisting of two rectangular volumes, arranged parallel to one another, but slightly displaced. Both are located along the slope of the land, and access is provided at the highest point. Starting from the vestibule, a ramp descends along the natural slope of the hill, leading the visitor to the living room and the large wooden patio at the other end of the house. The ramp then continues until it fades into the forest.

A second ramp leads up from the vestibule to the neighboring building. On the first floor is the bathroom, an unusually open room with panoramic views of the forest, the perfect spot to relax for hours in the bathtub. An exterior staircase leads from the contiguous patio to the wooden platform on the ground floor.

In this way, the house is arranged around a circular route which links the two floors and the interior to the patios. As in Iida's other project included in this book, the "O" Residence, the itinerary around the house is the axis of the house which determines the distribution and design of the other spaces.

Architecture can ignore time and be constructed from fixed, independent images. This is only possible, however, when it takes into account the pace, pauses, speed and itineraries of its inhabitants. It is only then that it transcends constructive logic, functional arrangement of rooms, and the purely visual and physical attributes of its volumes and becomes a harmonicous construction which invites the person who inhabits it to experience space in a richer, more complete, less arbitrary way.

In the largest room, which holds the vestibule, tatami room, dining room and living room, the various spaces are terraced according to the slope of the terrain and the ramp. It is in effect one large double-height room, with closed side walls, open at the front and back. At each end, a patio connects the interior with the forest.

Seen in this light, Yoshihiko Iida's project might be considered to be the simplest construction possible: little more than a couple of walls and a roof placed along one of the paths that cross the mountain with, at the side of the path, a modest refuge for sleeping and washing.

House in Tateshina

Yoshihiko Iida places a huge wooden platform at the front of the house. The platform has various levels and incorporates a double-height porch and sculptural outdoor staircase. The result is something like a public square in the middle of the forest.

 Site plan.

South elevation.

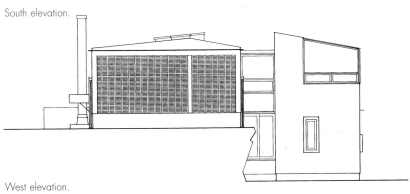

West elevation.

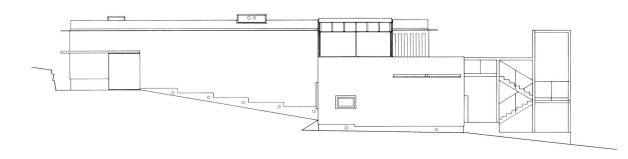

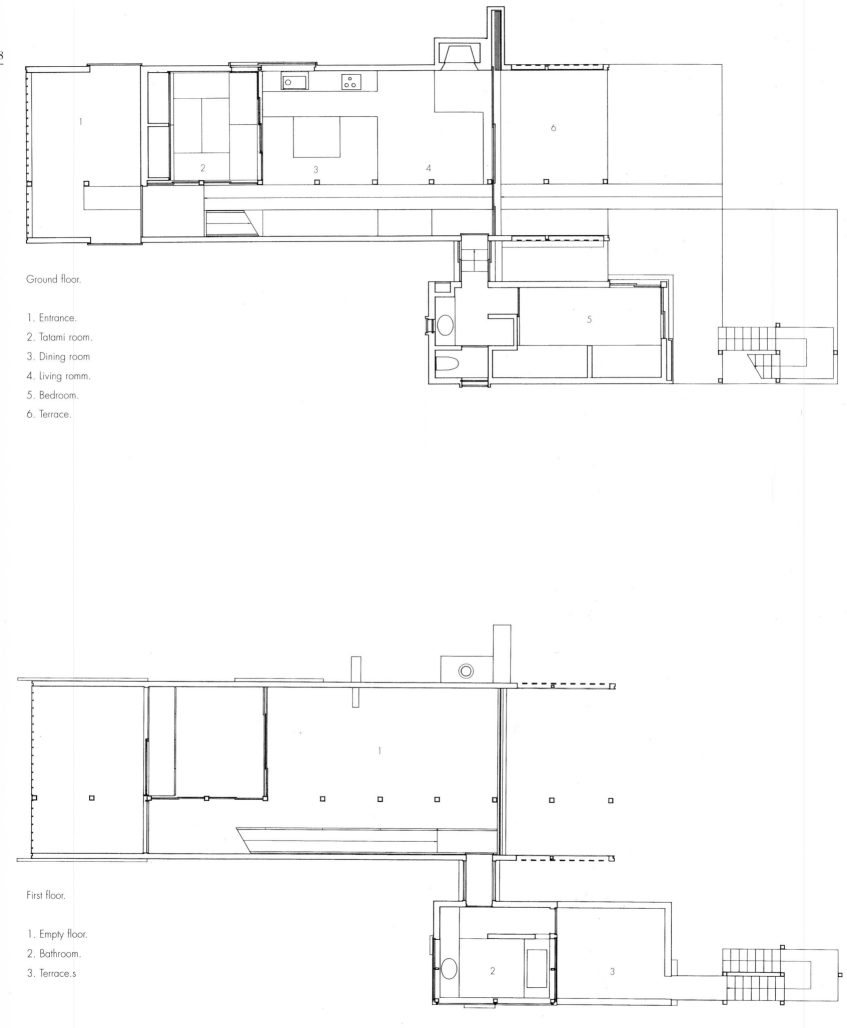

Ground floor.

1. Entrance.

2. Tatami room.

3. Dining room

4. Living romm.

5. Bedroom.

6. Terrace.

First floor.

1. Empty floor.

2. Bathroom.

3. Terrace.s

Both inside and outside the house, the material of choice is wood. In this way, the house is tonally and materially integrated into the surrounding forest.

The extensive use of wood to clad the walls and as the principal material for the furniture, along with the geometric simplicity of the space, give the living room an extraordinarily simple, contained image.

Longitudinal section, showing the elements which arrange the itinerary (on different levels) around which the house is organized: the two ramps and the stairway.

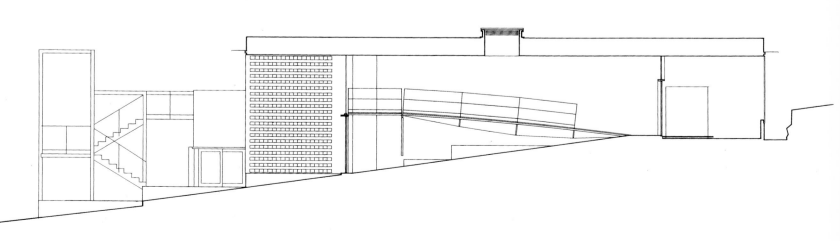

House in Tateshina

Location: Tateshina, Nagano, Japón.

Completion date: 1994.

Architect: Yoshihiko Iida.

Collaborator: Niitsu (constructor)

Photographer: Koumei Tanaka.

House in Tateshina House in Tateshina House in Tateshina House in Tateshina House in Tateshina House in Tateshina House in Tateshina House in Tateshina House in Tateshina House in Tateshina House in Tateshina House in Tateshina House in Tateshina

Patkau Architects

If your starting point is a site on Vancouver Island within a forested five acres, looking over the Strait of Georgia that divides the island from mainland Canada, many would ask how you could fail to create a beautiful home. Of course the resounding reply would be "in a million ways". Patkau Architects, fully aware of the natural beauty of British Columbia and its inevitable protagonism in the design, also fully aware of the pitfalls. There is a simple beauty in this project that indicates were that the thinking behind the design is very structured and studied. The architects' clarity of vision comes across in many ways: the luminous, fluid spaces, the fine details, the complex geometry of the timber roof.

The Vancouver-based architects confirm that the design of Barnes House is part of their current research based on three clear objectives: a search for the particular, a search for what is real and a search for heterogeneity. It is something of a reaction to post-modernism and the international bias of the modern movement.

The search for the particular as opposed to the general, is centered on the individual characteristics of the project: in this case it is the site, in its widest sense, including the whole region and figuratively speaking. The house is designed to enable its inhabitants to experience the place.

In their search for "the real", the architects consider the design should be based on what they are actually dealing with, not on some ideal. It is a more pragmatic approach. The topography of the site plays an important part. As Barnes House is built on an uneven, rocky outcrop, its structure is almost moulded to the land. It has an irregularity of form and variability of space and massing in common with the location. It nestles into the site, with the different levels incorporated into its plan. Man makes concessions to nature, and not vice versa. Entry to the house is on the lower floor, housing studio and guest bedroom, through the striking "prow"; stairs lead to the main floor, making a sequence of movement which reinforces this relation to the site. Living room, dining room, kitchen and master bedroom are all in this large expansive space. Here, with the surrounding conifers and extensive views, there is a sense of being in the tree tops.

The heterogeneous nature of the house is inevitable after seeking out what is particular and what is real. Barnes House manifests it in formal/spatial terms: the conjunction of orthogonal and non-orthogonal geometries; the figural strength of the north and west elevations set against a figural weakness in the south and east elevations; the enormous timber beams in contrast to the slender, elegant steel.

The house is expressive in its construction, using basic materials on the whole. The shell is a conventional wood frame, stucco clad, on a reinforced-concrete grade beam foundation. Three concrete columns rise up through both floors to support the heavy roof. The steel, as a more refined, prefabricated material, is used for detailed, more decorative work like the stair rail, joints and the canopy over the huge window in the living room and the entrance below.

Barnes House is a far cry from the traditional Canadian log cabin, but the huge timbers and variety of attractive wood seem to provide some recognition of the fact this is logging territory. As a counterpoint the extensive use of glass, the minimalist window details and the bold use of concrete make it unmistakably contemporary.

Barnes House

In Patkau architects, projects it is essential to acknowledge the "found potential", which in Barnes House was the site, without any doubt. "In this context the house has been designed as a landscape-focusing device – a mechanism through which the experience of this place, from the small-scaled textural characteristics of the rock to the large-scaled expanse of the sea, is made manifest."

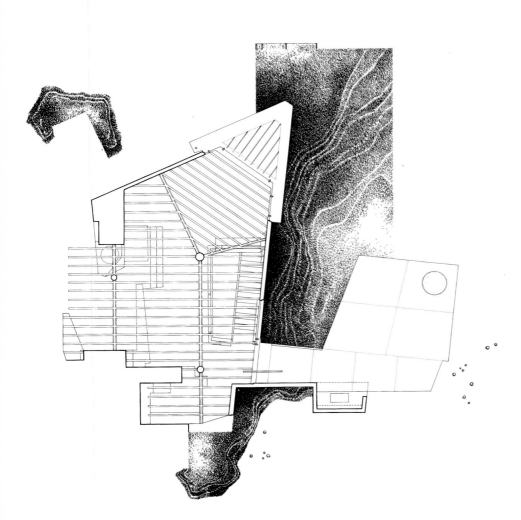

An elegant, simple window at the foot of the stairs reveals the details of a rock and emphasises the proximity and beauty of the earth, while the enormous window facing north west shows through the trees expansive stretches across the sea to mainland Canada.

The foundations are made of
reinforced-concrete grade beans,
and thee concrete columns rise up
through the house to support the
wooden roof.

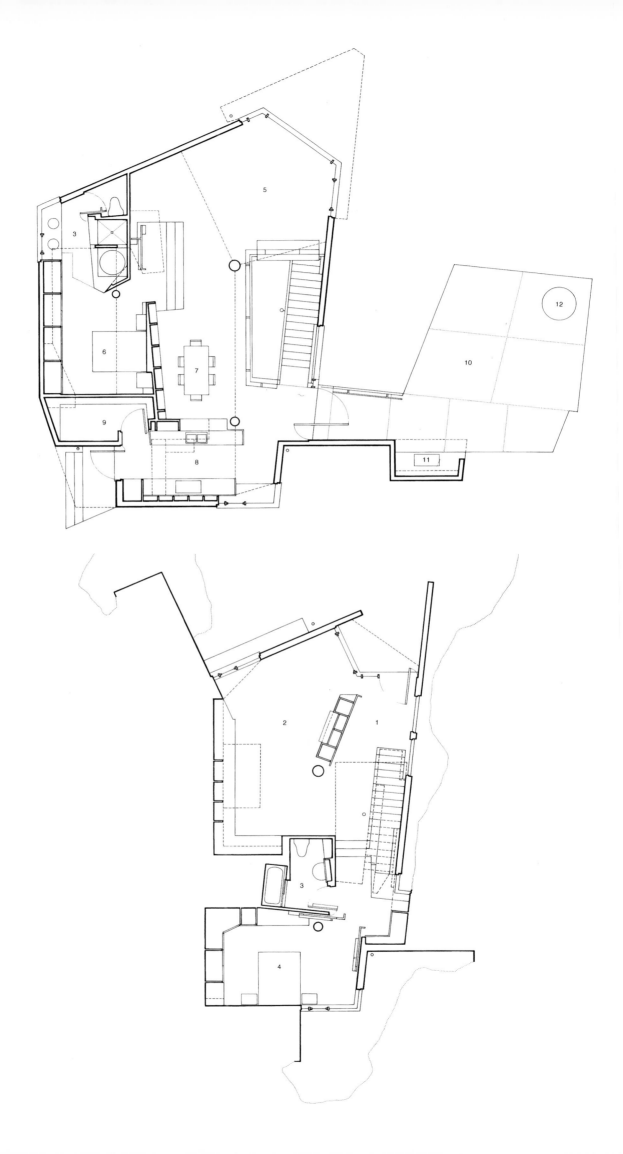

Lower floor.

1. Entry.

2. Studio.

3. Bathroom.

4. Guest room.

5. Living room.

6. Master bedroom.

7. Dining room.

8. Kitchen.

9. Utility Room.

10. Terrace.

11. Barbeque.

12. Firepit.

There is a generosity of space within the house, like another reference to the sweeping expanse outside. The stairwell is double its necessary width and despite the size, there are only two bedrooms.

View of the room and kitchen which are open to the living room. Behind is the main entrance and the staircase leading to the lower floor.

Two sections of the house showing clearly the slope of the land and the angular outline of the wooden roof.

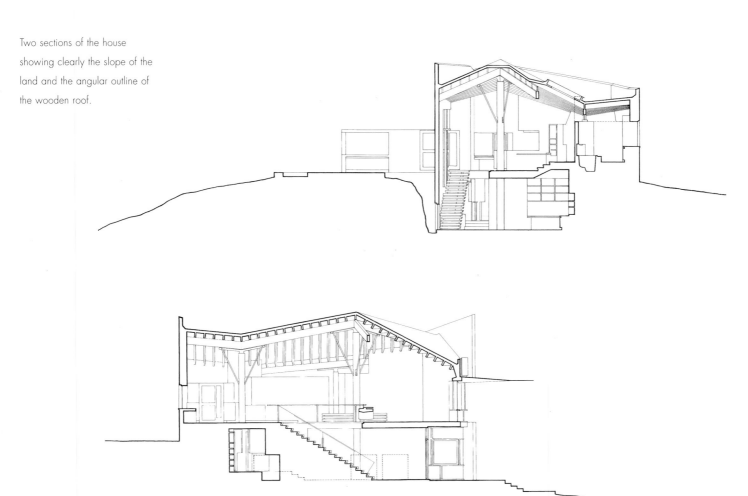

Various views of the upper floor.

Barnes House

Location: Nanaimo, British Columbia.

Completion date: 1993.

Architects: Tim Newton, John Patkau, Patricia Patkau, David Shone, Tom Robertson.

Collaborators: Fast & Epp Partners (structure), Robert Wall Ltd. (contractor).

Photographer: Undine Pröhl.

Type/Variant House

Vincent James

The type/Variant House is a 7,500 suare foot building set in the North Woods. It has a monumental, academic air as if it were on a university campus.

The fact architect Vincent James teaches at the University of Minnesota, and is known for his work on children's museums and other cultural buildings may have left its stamp. However the Type/Variant has been designed with a very different purpose: to be a lakeside summer home for a large family.

The fundamental idea behind the project actually came from James' clients who were fascinated by the concept of "Type/Variant". It can be interpreted as taking one "type" of object or being, and forming a collection of similar types, that are all slightly different from each other. The subtle differences between them create interesting relationships and as a composite whole they take on a different presence. The architect uses the analogy of a butterfly collection in a glass case: each one has an individual beauty, and the play between the similarities and differences gives the collection its aesthetic appeal.

Translated to the design of this home, the individual pieces are variations on the theme of a box. A series of wood - lined boxes, both horizontal and vertical, are placed orthogonally to each other and the house is derived from their composition. Even the outdoor spaces are designed within the same system. This design concept ties in with the client brief: a couple with five adult children wanting a vacation home for family gatherings: the individual members (with their own variants) can reunite here as one family.

Each space is allocated a size, shape and proportion according to its requirements both in mood and function; they respond to the rhythms and patterns of domestic life. Also the orientation and natural light is different in each space. The larger, living spaces and outdoor terraces on the upper floors are for communal activities, while the smaller spaces provide intimacy and solitude. The Douglas fir lining reinforces the quiet privacy in a comforting cave-like way, though it is not oppressive as the horizontal paneling guides the perspective outwards to the views through the window. There is even a space in total isolation for anyone who needs to break away (though still be linked to the group): a 24-foot high guest tower is set apart to the south of the main building.

The architect was anxious not to mimic the traditional rustic buildings that are the pride of the Upper Midwest, and treasured by the people from Chicago and the Twin Cities (St Paul and Minneapolis) who flock to this dramatically beautiful area for vacations. James sought inspiration in the more industrial buildings in the area, like granaries, valuing the "clear, strainightfforward quality to their construction" which comes from the direct relationship between their use and form. This also suited the clients who were keen to avoid rustic sentimentalism. The industrial edge is counterbalanced though by the warmth of the materials used: Douglas fir and bluestone are predominant in the interiors and the exterior walls are copper clad. These three are assembled in a variety of rhythmic patterns.

A key element in the design concept is the effect of time and weathering on the materials; the house will evolve over the years. The copper will change from its original pinkish - orange to blue and purple, a deep brown and then the bright green of verdigris. These subtle changes and the different shades of the bluestone harmonize with the textures, colors and seasonal changes in the natural surroundings. This striking Modernist house is by no means one of a type, but in its own particular way will grow and become an integral part of the North Woods.

Type/Variant House

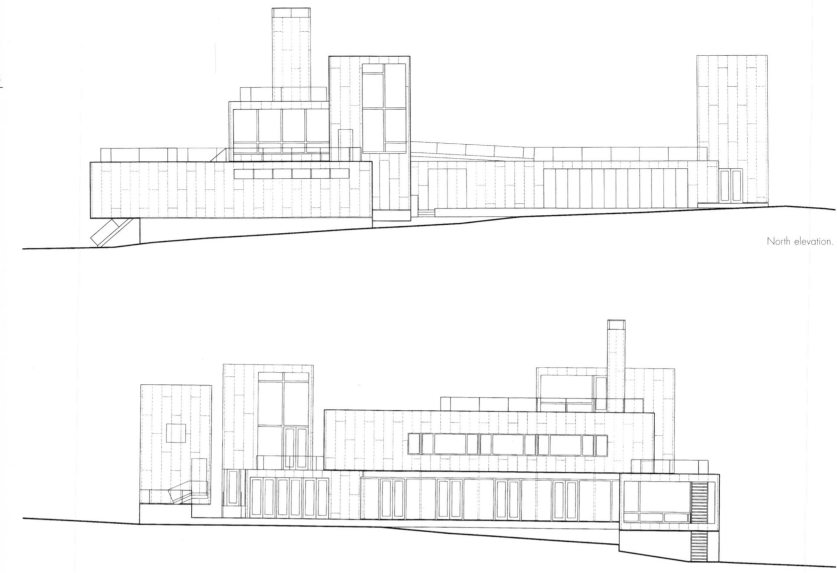

North elevation.

East elevation.

Architect and client worked closely together to develop the intriguing idea of the type/variant which forms the basic design concept behind this lakeside family home. An ambitious project that has resulted in a very contemporary looking building with a fascinating abstract quality.

South elevation.

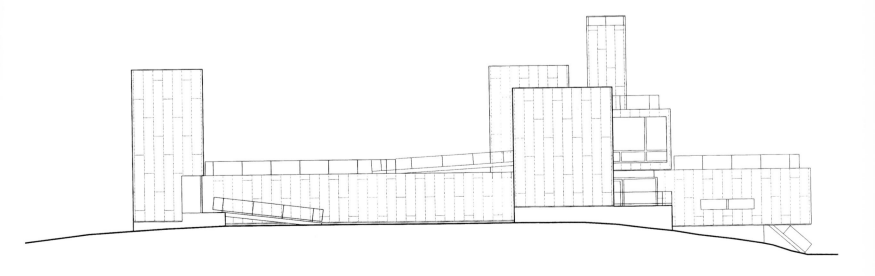

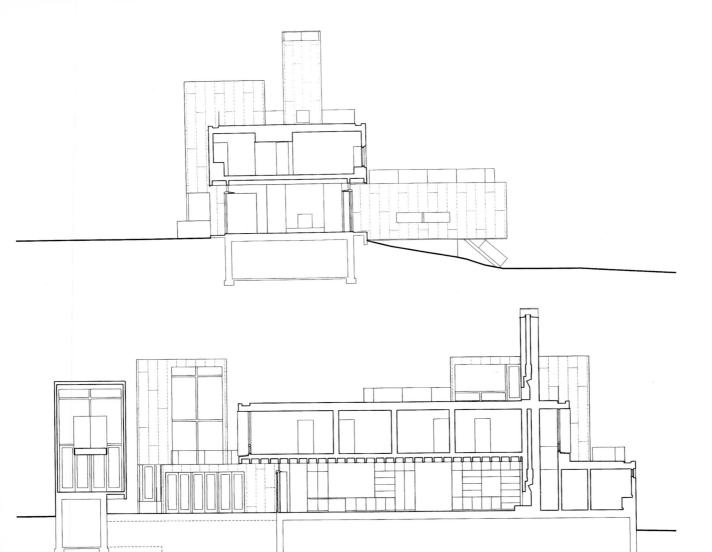

Between the different volumes there are many outdoor spaces half-enclosed and sheltered from the wind.

Transversal section looking north.

Longitudinal section looking west.

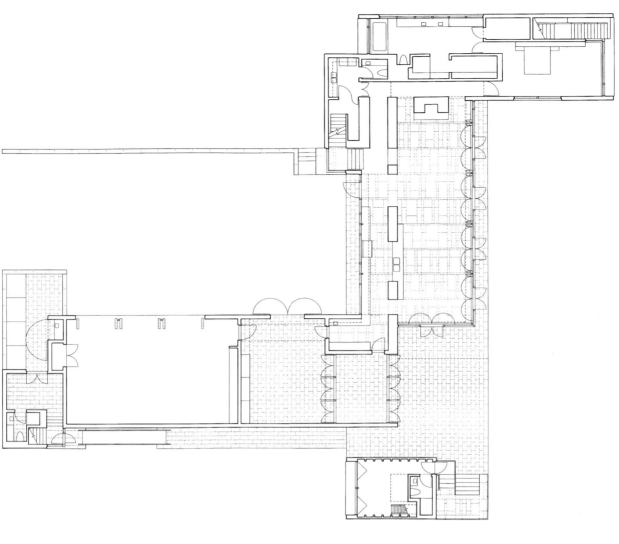

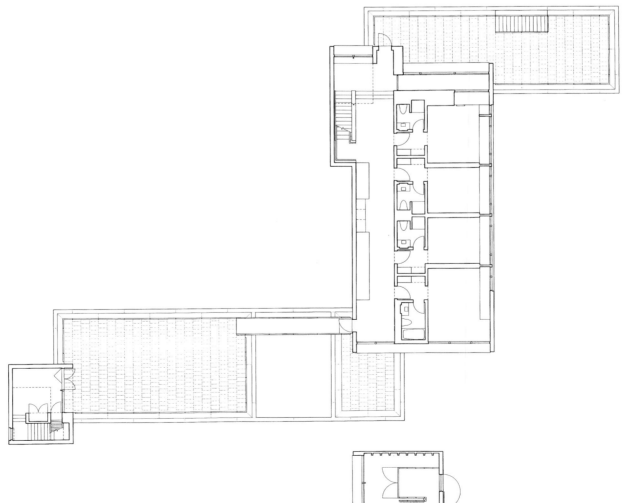

View of interior patio in the
south wing and the bridge which
runs across it. This patio is
located between the garage and
kitchen. The left-hand wall has
been lined with logs for the fire.

Third floor.

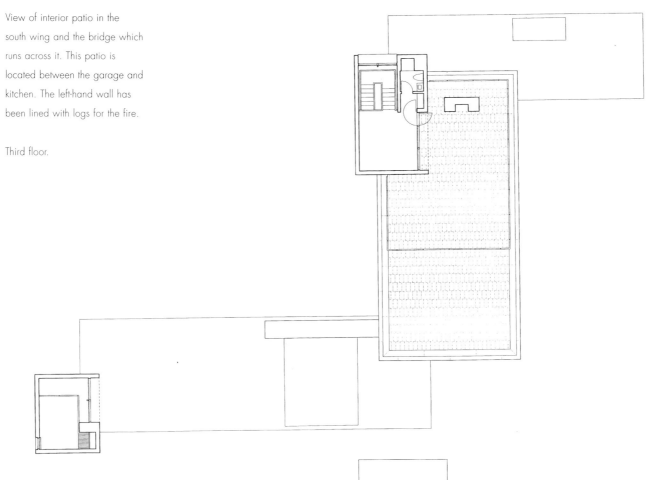

These axonometries show now
the different bodies of the
house have an interplay
volumetrically.

Building section for living
room and bedroom module.

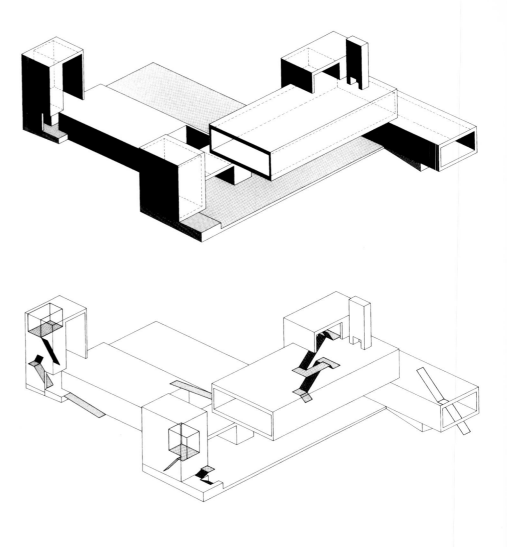

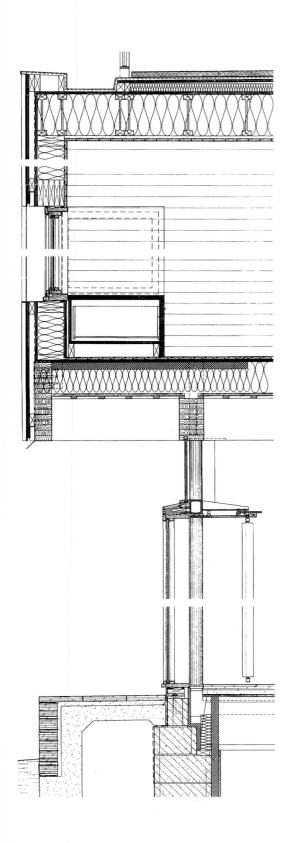

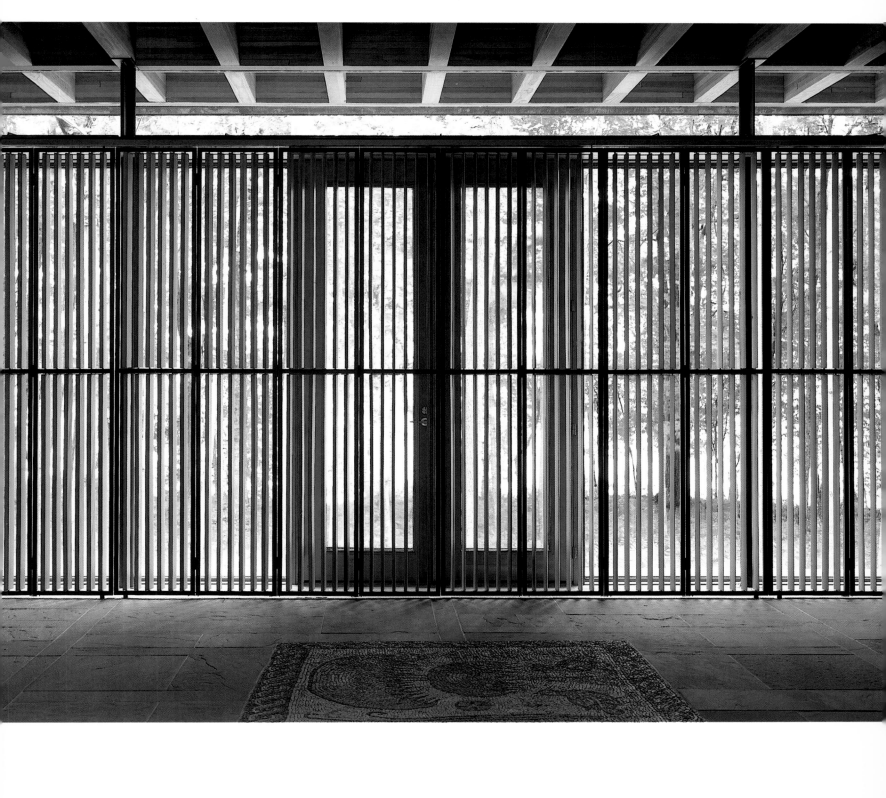

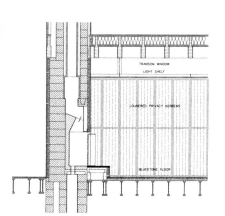

TRANSOM WINDOW
LIGHT SHELF

LOUVERED PRIVACY SCREENS

BLUESTONE FLOOR

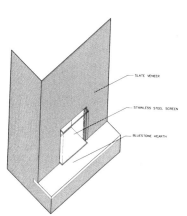

SLATE VENEER

STAINLESS STEEL SCREEN

BLUESTONE HEARTH

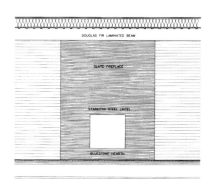

DOUGLAS FIR LAMINATED BEAM

SLATE FIREPLACE

STAINLESS STEEL LINTEL

BLUESTONE HEARTH

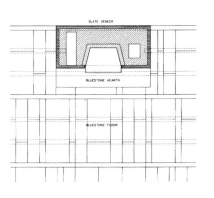

SLATE VENEER

BLUESTONE HEARTH

BLUESTONE FLOOR

Type/Variant House

Location: Wisconsin, U.S.A.

Date of construction: 1996.

Architects: Vincent James, Paul Yaggie.

Collaborators: Nancy Blanfard, Nathan Knuston, Andrew Dull, Steve Lazen, Krista Scheib, Julie Snow, Taavo Somer, Kate Wyberg (design), Coen + Stumpf and Associates (landscape), Yerigan Construction (contractor).

Photographer: Don F. Wong.

iant House
e/Variant House
/Variant
it House
e Type/Variant House
Variant House
House
ouse Type/Variant House
Variant House
int House
House Type/Variant House
House Type/Variant House
t House
Variant House